Lost in Japan

I0132674

The

Complete Series

1st EDITION

Daniel R. Larson

Acknowledgments

My brother, Eric — For working to help me find a way to get Kazuki and Mae out of Japan. He is a true and strong Navy man.

American Service Officer Taylor — For his personal dedication to returning Kazuki and Mae to American soil, far beyond the call of duty.

My mother, Rosalie — For her support, given with every bit of strength. She is the strongest person I will ever know.

My father, Rick — For funding travel, for a lifetime of dedication to excellence in the written word, and for telling me more times than I can count, "If you want to do it, figure it out."

My attorney, Jolene — For doing everything within her power to try to keep Kazuki and Mae in the United States — twice.

Lisa DelleDonne — For cheering me on every single day when I was alone in Japan.

Beth Kost — For being the best neighbor, and for helping me raise the kids.

My aunt, Nelle Patterson — For being there for us when we needed her most.

Leah Velasquez — For having me in her awesome St. Paul basement while traveling between Minneapolis and Tokyo.

Karly McMillen— For making me laugh, even when it was not funny.

Charles Johnson — For supporting me unconditionally, and for going through my divorce as though Kazuki and Mae were his own.

Mark Vogel — For introducing me to the mother of my two children and the enriching world of nature, food, and culture that is Japan.

My brother, Greg — For providing the framework to make this book series possible.

Contents

Contents

Contents

Editorial Notes

The author and Larson Publishing make no assertion that conversations happened exactly as depicted. Conversations, instead, accurately illustrate circumstances at the times they are depicted.

In some instances, information depicted as acquired through a single conversation, was — in fact — acquired through a series of conversations, or personal research.

Some details are impressionistic, rather than literal, in order to illustrate the impact of circumstances and events.

The author and Larson Publishing acknowledge that many depicted circumstances and events are emotionally charged and that accounts may vary.

The author and Larson Publishing acknowledge that all parties were in difficult situations, and that all parties did the best they could with the resources they had available at the time.

This book is not intended to cause harm or injury to any involved parties. The author and Larson Publishing regret any unintentional harm or injury resulting from the publishing and marketing of the Lost in Japan series.

The author and Larson Publishing assert that public awareness of all systematic devaluation — and corresponding denial or diminishment of — fathers' rights is in the public's interest.

Some names have been changed or withheld in order to preserve privacy.

PROLOGUE

序章

"*I*'m taking the kids and moving to Japan —"

My Japanese wife Miya (Me-ya) dropped it on me, staring me down for my reaction.

It was September 18th of 2011, and we stood – arms crossed, three feet away from each other – in the living room of our 1200 square foot, first-floor condo.

As she peered through me, I looked past her at the earth tone walls we'd painted together.

I turned my head away from her peering eyes and stared through the double-pane sliding glass door.

In our backyard, the brown and gold autumn leaves swirled in the wind against the muddy suburban grass and the gray Plymouth, Minnesota sky.

She'd been threatening to run to Japan since she'd been pregnant with our son Kazuki (Kah-zoo-key) in 2004, but this had last reached a breaking point when she'd been eight months pregnant with Mae (May) back in 2006.

Back then, she'd smashed our Chinaware into the kitchen floor, run to the living room, dropped to the carpet, and pounded her fists, screaming.

"I'm *not gonna* stay home with two kids! Kazuki can't even fall asleep by himself. I need my mom's help!"

Standing in the kitchen, looking at the smashed shards of glass all over the floor, I'd given her my last best option.

"Miya, I can change my work schedule and stay home with the kids."

Miya had retorted, sitting in a heap, her head down, combing through her two feet of black hair with her fingers.

"If you can't really do it, I'll have *an abortion*."

I had sat down on the tan carpeted floor next to her.

"No Miya. You can't. That's my baby too. Nobody aborts an eight-month pregnancy."

She'd looked up at me.

"You're so *stupid*. I can even do it myself. Nobody will ever even know."

I had put my face in my hands and looked out at her through my fingers.

"I'll change my schedule... I'll do all the kids' stuff, okay?"

Then, she'd pulled her shedding hair out in clumps, as though milking a cow. She'd sifted it through her fingers, laying the long, black clumps of hair in a pile on that light tan carpet.

Tears and mascara and sweat all over her face, she'd said, "If you don't really do it, and I have this baby, I'm taking the kids and moving to Japan. You *can't stop* me."

So... I did it. After Mae was born in late 2006, I had changed my schedule so that I could be home with the kids. And my relieving Miya *had* made her happy... for a while.

But, after a few years, Miya had started asking me to change my schedule again so that she could stay home with the kids.

I had refused –

Dressing and bathing and cooking and housework; she would have started raging again that she'd run to Japan for her mom's help.

And so, here we were. It was September 18th of 2011, and Miya had just told me that she was taking our kids to Japan.

I walked over to her – her arms crossed – and put my hands on her shoulders.

"Miya, what are you talking about? Are you really doing this?"

She squinted and pulled back.

"I gave two weeks-notice at work and bought three one-way tickets."

Apparently, she really was doing this.

I said, "Where will you go?"

She backpedaled toward the front door, crossing her arms in fists over her chest.

"We are moving to my parents' house in Misato."

She glared into the entryway closet.

"You can come too... if you want."

I said, "Wait... what? Are you serious?"

She dug through that entryway closet, then peaked her head out and hissed at me.

"My mom said to *make sure* that I get the kids. She doesn't care if you come with or not."

Miya came back into the living room with a fruit shipping box and threw clothes and toys into it, as if to *show* me that she was really leaving.

I said, "Listen, I know you're not happy about living in the United States, but – *please* – let's try to work this out. Our *whole lives* are here."

She threw a sparkly stuffed unicorn into the totally-not-international-travel-ready cardboard box.

"I don't care. I hate America, you never help with dishes or anything. You never even take care of your kids – and you're not willing to work."

I walked over to her as she threw clothes and stuffed toys into a box, trying to make eye contact.

"Miya, I get the kids to school. I'm working whenever you're not. I'm trying to do a lot of things here."

She threw down a stuffed bear, rushed to me, and stuck her finger in my face.

"I don't care your *stupid excuses* anymore. *We'll go to Japan.* You decide if you're going to help me pack, or if you're gonna *try and stop me.*"

The next day, after dropping the kids off at school, I went to my attorney's tenth floor Bloomington office.

My attorney, Jolene, whisked platinum-blond hair off her left shoulder, taking a moment to think.

"Well," she said, "you could sue for divorce and request a court order keeping the kids in Minnesota, but that court order would *not actually stop Miya from taking the kids and leaving.*"

Sitting across from her at her wide wooden desk, I shook my head.

"What?"

She stood up, and looked – with her steely blue eyes – out the window, and pointed across the grid locked interstate.

"There are no means for upholding orders at that airport," she said.

Then she looked down, pulling at the bottom of her black suitcoat. It matched her black pants and her high black heels.

She looked back at me.

"America has no exit controls. You can't stop her from going…"

She walked toward her desk, touching her hand to her gold necklace.

"And if Miya does take the kids to Japan," she said, "there will be nothing that anybody here can do."

I put my left hand to my forehead, then flipped it at her.

"That makes no sense. Is it *nothing*? Does that really mean *nothing*?"

She sat down across from me, at that mahogany desk, in her black leather chair.

"You have to understand the ramifications that Japan is not a member of the Hague Convention," she said, "It's the international treaty for child abduction. Japan is *not* a member."

I squinted, staring at her.

She crossed her arms.

"Dan... kids taken there on one-way tickets don't come back."

I shook my head in defiance.

"Holy shit. Hold on – so, we can't stop her from leaving, and if she goes, we can't get the kids *back*?"

She curled her lip and nodded.

I said, "What? So, what are we *doing* here?"

She leaned into me, her hands flat on that desk.

"I mean, Minnesota could issue her an arrest warrant if she violated an order keeping the kids here, but so what?"

Now she leaned back, throwing up her hands.

"Her whole plan is to leave the United States. In that case, she might even say that it was *your fault* that she couldn't come back to Minnesota *because* of that arrest warrant. And – I don't know – but I think the Japanese courts could step in to protect her, or they could just do nothing at all."

That mahogany desk suddenly looked so heavy.

"I really hate having to be reactive about this," I said, crossing my arms over my chest and tapping – repeatedly – my right biceps with my left index finger, "You make is sound as if I have no options."

She leaned into me again, from across her heavy, dark-finish stained mahogany desk.

"No. It's not that you have no options; it's that you have no *good* options."

I leaned back in her black leather office chair.

"So, what am I supposed to do?"

She looked down at her yellow notepad, tapping a Bic pen.

"I would not agree to go there for more than six months, "she said, "There's something called UCCJEA. The United States courts have to honor the kids' residence for the past six months. If the kids were in Japan for longer, the court here could interpret that their new habitual residence was in Japan."

I stared at her.

She snapped her fingers and pointed at me.

"I want you to promise that you will contact an attorney in Japan, and ask them how they might be able to help."

I covered my eyes with my left hand.

"*That's* your idea for what I'm supposed to do?"

"Daniel," she said, "this situation has all the makings of an international crisis."

I got home from work at 10:30 that night, opened the old wooden door to our condo, and found two four-foot-square cardboard boxes in our living room. Both the shipping boxes were half-full of the kids' clothes and toys. Next to them were two luggage bags and a duffle bag, all half-full. And strewn across our light-tan living room carpet were more clothes and toys. It looked like a garage sale had thrown up all over the place.

I made a face like I'd bitten into a lemon and ran back out to my Saturn Vue.

I googled *Japan international custody* and found a Tokyo attorney named Tanase 棚瀬孝雄 (Tah-nah-say).

Speaking slowly, he said, "Ours is not a modern legal system. Your wife can come here and just *affirm* her custody of your kids, because all three of them are Japanese citizens and you are not."

Sitting in that silver Saturn Vue in front of my suburban condo, I felt my arms and legs shaking.

"What? How can that be?"

"In Japan," he said, "citizenship is by blood, not birth location. For Japan, your kids will be like life-long residents coming home."

I wanted to smash my phone into the pavement. Instead, I gripped it tightly.

"But they were born and raised in Minnesota. They've never even lived in Japan."

"Yes, I understand," he said.

His calm voice offended me.

I tried again.

"So, what if I just stash the kids' passports until we get this resolved?"

He paused – then said, "Would she be willing to check a box stating that you are abusive, in order to take the kids to Japan?"

I thought of that snowy December day in 2004 when my son was born. That day, he had made me who I was; he had made me a father.

I said, "Of course she would. She already tells her Japanese friends that I'm abusive."

He paused again – then said, "I am not surprised. It happens all the time. She can say 'DV' by a foreigner, and everybody in Japan will believe her."

I said, "DV?"

He cleared his throat.

"Domestic Violence; it is a big issue in Japan. She can say 'DV,' providing no evidence, and she will be believed. It is because you are a man, but it is especially worse because you are a foreigner. They will even hide her address from you."

I huffed an exasperated exhale.

I said, "I know where she's going. She's going to her parents' house in Misato. They're not trying to keep me from there."

He said, "Ah, good. That's good. But, if you decide to try to stop her from leaving – even if you have their passports – that is no protection at all. The Japanese Embassy will easily replace those without your ever even knowing. She can even have the new passports rushed to her because it is a *family emergency*."

I said, "Because she can claim DV?"

He said, "Exactly."

I squeezed my temples with my hand, trying to relieve the pressure in my skull.

"So, I truly don't know what to do here. She gave leave notice with her employer and bought one-way tickets to Narita."

He said, "Ah so, I suggest that you consider your next move very carefully. Any choice you make from now could end your parental rights."

I closed my flip phone, and – my car, my driveway, and all of outside went black.

A week later I called a meeting, hoping somebody could reason with Miya.

It was:

Two Minnesotan couples from the suburbs; four of Miya's female Japanese friends; my father, who had flown in from Florida; and Miya's mother Akiko, who got on the phone.

I had set up a circle of chairs and our two couches, but the four Japanese women all sat together on the floor, against the wall.

My father stood up and gave it a try.

"Miya, you are making picking up a family and moving to the other side of the planet, where your husband doesn't speak the language, sound reasonable. When you guys got married, it was here in Minnesota. This was not part of the deal."

Miya's friend, Hitomi, stood up.

"My American husband — sorry to say, but just like Dan — is also not willing to work or help raise our kids. I feel it is some cultural issue that American men are not willing to work hard enough. He also blames me for his laziness. I am also thinking of taking our kids to Japan. I think, if I can get enough support, he also cannot stop me."

She sat back down on the floor, wiping tears from her face, as her words landed with a thud. The room drew to total silence, and the Japanese women all turned to her, nodding and bowing as they sat on their feet.

I looked at my father, sitting next to me, then turned and looked at the people sitting across my living room.

"*I have a job*. I have *always* had a job, since the day I met Miya. I'll start working full-time again, but then somebody is going to have to take care of our kids. That means packing lunches; getting them to school; getting them dressed; getting them to dance and karate – not just complaining about *how* I do it, or saying that I will not do it *while* I'm doing it. Somebody is going to have to *actually* do it."

Miya turned on her chair to the Japanese women sitting seiza 正座 (butt to heals) against the wall next to the front door. She produced a smile.

"See, this is what I mean. He always says some excuse. What he is saying is the reason I need help from my mom."

A chorus rose up to discuss in Japanese.

I turned to my father and whispered.

"Since when is explaining something an excuse?"

He leaned into me, sitting on the old wooden chair next to the light-tan leather couch where I sat, and whispered.

"You don't seem to understand; you *cannot* let her do this."

I looked him dead in the eye for the first time I could remember.

"No, *you* don't understand; I *can't stop her*."

He looked away and grimaced.

"You have to try."

I made a fist with my right hand, hit it against my right leg, and whispered an enraged whisper.

"If I try, she could take the kids and they could be gone *forever*."

My father looked back at me with a glint in his eye I will never be able to explain. I could see his world crashing in.

The room quieted down.

Miya's mother, Akiko, pleaded through the speaker phone.

"This is your chance to take care of your wife. I didn't even want her to marry you because she is gone, in America. It is too long. It is time to make it even. Dan, why can't you sacrifice yourself?"

I looked at my father, who was gently shaking his head, "no."

The next day, Miya and I sat at our kitchen table. Having exhausted all my options, I pitched her an offer.

"Miya, I will agree that you can go, but you have to agree, in writing, to return to Minnesota – either to move back home, or for a visit – within six months."

She looked at me sheepishly and nodded.

"Okay."

I wrote it down, and we both signed it:

Miya is to take Kazuki and Mae to Japan on October 3rd. Dan will stay in Minnesota for an additional month to sell off our stuff and rent out our condo.

Dan will meet Miya, Kazuki, and Mae in Misato in early November.

We are all to return to Minnesota on or before April 2nd, 2012 –

TOKYO

東京

Lost in Tokyo

東京 *1*

I landed in Narita, Japan 成田日本 on November

1st of 2011, hoping that it was the first day of the last opportunity to hold my family together, knowing that I was in for the battle of my life.

I took the escalator down into the train station below the airport, and caught the train to Tokyo Station 東京駅. 90 minutes later, I arrived.

As I stepped off that Narita-to-Tokyo train, it really settled in – all-at-once – that this would be my first time in Tokyo without Miya talking to people, reading signs, buying tickets, exchanging money, and telling me where I was. My English was about to become worthless.

I was suddenly engulfed in hundreds of Japanese rushing out of the train and onto a concrete platform as a woman barked in muffled Japanese over some loudspeaker. I was swept down an escalator, and down a white hallway. I turned the corner, left, and the place opened up into the busiest train station in the world. Somehow, physics seemed to break down as the underground roof shot three stories overhead, and eight hallways seemed to split out of four corners.

What am I looking at? Where the hell am I? Try to stay calm.

There was a mascot bear selling a convenience store, a robot selling insurance, shouting teenagers selling noodles, a raw fish restaurant, cosmetics for men, and drunken men stumbling around in suits. And my map seemed to say it was all tied together by a spaghetti plate of train lines.

Miya's utopian ideal was smashing right into my reality –

I bolted through the wide hallway, then put my back to a giant white pillar, the underground ceiling somehow 30-feet overhead, as thousands of Tokyoites rushed past in every direction.

What have I done? I'm so lost. This is like Mars. Okay, don't lose your head. You've gotta find your way out of this station.

I flipped through my pages of computer-printed pictures, directions, and physical markers. I took off my glasses and squinted.

None of this looks right –

I darted to a train ticket booth and asked a man in a blue uniform how to get to my bullet train.

He said, 「直進、左折。その後、右折します。」

Oh great. Now I'm Chris Farley in a Saturday Night Live skit.

Mother of Mercy, I don't speak Japanese!

The mid-day heat blasted through the station corridors as I bolted up and down escalators – past bakeries, past liquor stores, and past convenience stores – looking for my train to Misato.

I was unable to tell if each were a new spot, or if I was spinning in circles.

Finally, a young woman from an information booth walked me to the bullet train ticket office. She brought me to a middle-aged man in what looked like a blue cruise ship captain's uniform.

He said, 「右手に角を回って行きます。列車は廊下です。」

Then he raised his cupped, white-gloved hand at a sign which read:

⇦❸❶②7834⑨⇨

My stomach sank.

A few hours ago, I was an educated, condo-owning, respected, real estate law instructor. Suddenly I'm an illiterate nobody foreigner with no home, no friends, and no job. And for what? For a woman who hates me.

I found the train platform, dragged my luggage up the escalator, found the wingless-jet-looking-bullet-train-thing, then still had to find my seat.

When I sat down, I thought of my only purpose: Kazuki and Mae. I hadn't seen them in a month. It was the longest I had ever gone without seeing them, and it had felt like forever.

Then, as the train pulled away from Tokyo Station and darted through that black tunnel, I shook my head and thought.

How the hell did I end up here? –

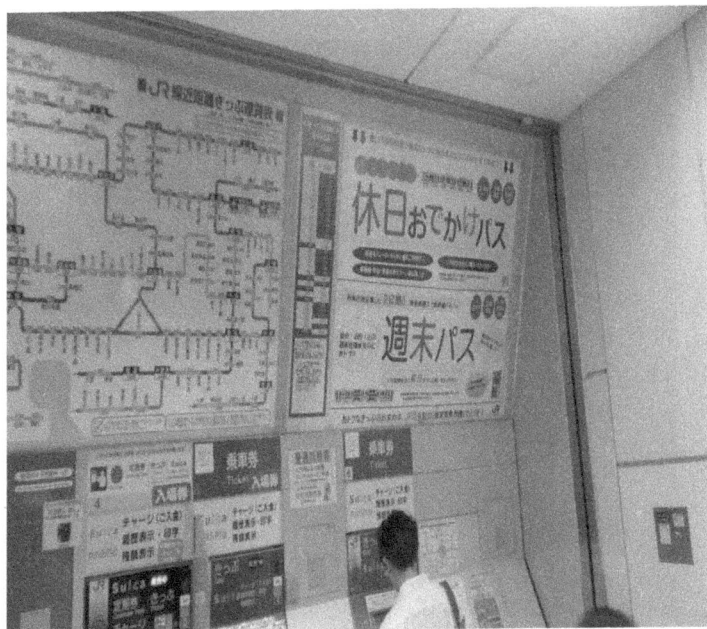

MINNESOTA

ミネソタ

Blind Date

2

*I*stood in an old Saint Cloud State University

bowling alley on February 16th of 2002.

My friend from high school, Mark, looked at me
and extended his arm.

"This is my girlfriend, Ayako. And this is her friend,
Miya."

Miya

美哉

*W*ow. *She is gorgeous.*

I extended my right hand.

She dropped her head and bowed to me.

I looked over at Mark, then back at Miya, and nodded.

"Hi, I'm Dan."

"Dahm?" she said.

I laughed and retracted my right hand.

"Dan. I'm Dan."

She said, "Oh! Don. Don."

I smiled and nodded.

"Yeah, that'll work."

So… we went bowling.

Miya walked past Mark and Ayako and me, pranced up to the line, and released the scuffed pink bowling ball. The jagged ball slowly ambled down the lane.

I sat, tying my shoes, looking over at her.

She was wearing these dark blue jeans with sparkly things on the back pockets, and this navy-blue top. There was white lace around her sleeves and a flower thing around the collar, and it flared out at the bottom. I had never seen anything like that in my life.

Her black hair shined, and she had these high cheekbones.

The ball rolled into the gutter. Then, Miya sat down and smiled at me, tucking her black hair behind her ear.

There was something different about her eyes. I didn't know… something… something.

The four of us went out for pizza off campus, where they attended school, and I did not.

I was so amped, in a hormone-induced scramble, trying to find some way to impress this woman.

I tried my best to serenade her.

"Pokémon! Gotta catch 'em all! Pokémon!"

Then, I leaned in.

"Do you like chow mein?"

She put her hand over her mouth and laughed.

"What's a chow thing? Like a cow? Chow grass?"

We all leaned back and laughed.

I don't know how I pulled it off, but at the end of the night, she gave me her phone number.

I called Miya in the middle of the following week.

"How are you?"

She sounded like she was reading from a book.

"Yes. Good."

"What's going on up there?" I said.

She said, "Hm. Yes. I think so."

I said, "You want me to come see you this weekend?"

She said, "Hm. Yes. I think so."

I hung up.

Wow. She does not speak English.

Well, at least all the yeses mean more dates.

I started driving an hour northwest from my folks' place in Minneapolis to Saint Cloud State every weekend.

I was 24 years old –

I... Don't... Have

3

*I*n the spring of 2002, the real estate market

was booming all over the country. So, right after meeting Miya, I decided to get my real estate license. I took the class in a Bloomington office park, across the street from the Mall of America, with over 100 other people.

The first day, a man came out in a suit and tie, stood on a platform, and shouted.

"Are you guys ready to get this license, and sell the American Dream?"

The crowd shouted back with hoots and hollers and whistles. Eight hours later, he got a standing ovation.

Wow, I though*t, forget sales. I wanna do that.*

So, I attended a training session in early April, hoping to perform seminars with this company.

On a mid-April Wednesday, I took a break from my training, and called Miya from the customer service landline.

"Should I come up there Friday night?"

There was a pause.

She muttered.

"I… don't… have."

I looked down at my textbook, poring over presentational notes and diagrams.

"Huh? What?"

"I… don't… have," she whispered, "Huh? Nani? Chigaimasu 違います. I… don't… care. I don't care."

My mentor, Dave – the guy who'd given that presentation to 100 people a few months earlier – walked past, and pounded me on the back.

"Dan-O!"

I pointed at him.

"Nice mustache."

He shot a crooked grin, ran his index finger across that dark brown mustache, and marched into the seminar room. Then, he waved me in.

I went back to Miya on the phone.

"What are you saying?"

"I don't care… you come or not," she whispered, "I don't care."

"Okay," I said, "why?"

"You say you help me study nursing," she said, "You don't do it."

"Alright," I said, "I gotta go."

After that, she didn't answer my calls for two weeks.

Then, in early May, she called me at my parents' house.

She said, "Will you please come help me study?"

I remembered that shirt, that hair… those eyes.

"I'll come up on Friday," I said.

So, Miya and I sat in the basement of that house she was renting in Saint Cloud, cozied up next to each other at the edge of her bed.

I said, "Hey Miya, this nursing license you're trying to get – don't you think it's too hard?"

She shook her head.

"No – I don't know. Why?"

I flipped through her textbook, as we sat on that red bed sheet on that mattress.

"I mean, *I* don't even know what these words mean."

I stopped on a random page and pointed.

"Ob-dor-mition – like, what does that mean?"

She paused for a few seconds, staring at the page.

"I don't know... I think it's arm tingle."

I closed the book.

"How are you going to learn this stuff?"

She said, "You promised to help me... you don't do it."

I said, "No, I'll do it. I'm just saying... How long before you're supposed to graduate?"

She said, "Two years."

I shook my head, pointing at a random page.

"And how long does it take you to read one page of this stuff?"

She said, "Like, one hour. I have to read five times."

I said, "It just seems hard is all."

She looked down.

"I came here to get American nursing license. I want to travel the world and help kids."

I tapped the book with the back of my fingers.

"But it's not working. How many times have you taken this class?"

She looked at me like a sad puppy.

"I'm gonna fail and have to do again. It's gonna be three times."

I said, "Okay, so I'm just saying – Why don't you get an easier degree?"

She stared at me.

"You said you help me."

I wrapped my arms around her.

"I'm *trying* to."

She said, "Okay, I'll cook for you now."

In mid-June, I did my first real estate seminar.

I stood up and said, "Okay! Who's ready to get this license and sell the American dream?"

My belt buckle fell apart and the belt popped open.

I looked down, then looked back up.

100 people stared at me in silence. A big man with a gray beard in the front row sat back and crossed his arms.

Afterward, I called Miya from that customer service line.

She said, "How did that go?"

I said, "Bad."

She said, "Um… how bad?"

I said, "*Really* very bad. I did a really bad seminar."

She said, "Hm. Okay. So, now what?"

"I don't know," I said, "I feel like I want to quit."

She said, "No, you don't quit. That's your thing you want to do. It's job. You can do."

I said, "Are you sure? I just… I don't know if I can pull this off."

She said, "I think you keep working on it. You can do."

That Friday, I went back up to campus and brought Miya out to that pizza place.

I pounded my fist on the table.

"What if… you stop struggling with those nursing classes, and we switch you over to that specialized B.A. with no major? I did some research. This school offers it."

She looked down at the table.

"What does that mean?"

I said, "I mean, you're struggling with your classes. If you switch your degree, you can graduate in six months, and I can help you study for those easier classes."

Silence.

She finally looked at me.

"So... I don't get nursing license?"

"No," I said, grabbing a piece of pizza from a raised pan, "I've got my career going... so."

She smiled.

"Your belt fell off."

I laughed.

"Yeah, but I'll get better. I can do it."

She patted the top of my hand.

"I came to America to get American nurse degree and travel to Africa or something with UNICEF. I want to work for kids. You know it."

"Well," I said, "you don't have to go to Africa. You could stay here... with me"

She looked across the tables throughout the restaurant.

"I have my student visa. It's legal issue. I'll have to go home – to Japan."

I put my arm around her, pulled her in, and bumped our foreheads together.

"If you're married to an American, you could stay here. You can get a spousal visa."

She swatted my shoulder.

"It's public. We don't supposed to touch each other."

I dropped cash on the table, took her by the hand, and bolted toward the front door.

I looked back to her.

"By the way, what do you want for your birthday?"

Those light brown eyes opened wide.

"I want a ring!"

On July 25th of 2002, under a high blue sky, in the grass at Saint Cloud State, I gave my Japanese-foreign-exchange-student-girlfriend a .75 carat princess cut diamond on a gold band.

She ran around the campus lawn, laughing at how the rock flashed in the sunlight.

I had known her for four months –

JAPAN

日本

Bullet Train to Misato

美郷電車 4

I tried to shake the memories out of my head as

the bullet train launched me out of the black
Tokyo Station tunnel and into the city above. I
blasted past gray apartments, glassy-blue
skyscrapers, flashing red bar lights, a thousand
tan houses, and a spider's web of black electrical
wires.

Suddenly, Tokyo 東京 melted into green trees and
brown rice fields.

For just a moment, I could clearly see Kazuki and
Mae's little faces. I could see them playing in the
woods next to our home in Minnesota. I could
hear them laughing –

I stood up as the train caromed down the rusted
rural tracks. I walked down the isle – past the
sleeping old man with his beer cracked open and

his chair laid back, past the sleeping little girl and her beautiful mother, holding hands – to the brown plastic faux-wooden door at the front of the car. It automatically opened upon my arrival. I ambled through the gangway, past the shelves of neatly-stashed luggage, to the urinal. I opened the bathroom door, walked into the two-foot-wide space, and grabbed the handle – jostled by the train.

I looked in the tiny mirror to my right, just above the tiny sink, with that tiny bathroom door behind me. I looked at my short brown hair and how it had thinned around the temples since Miya and I had been those kids running around that Saint Cloud State campus. I ran my hand down my face, feeling the rough, black stubble on my cheeks. I looked at the wrinkles around my eyes. I patted my chest with an open hand; it felt strong, even against my pounding heart. Two kids, and all these years later – I still looked pretty damn good.

Bounced every direction, against the physics of the train, I tried to amp myself up. It was not working. I had never felt so alone in my life.

I returned to my reserved seat, leaned it back, and did what most were doing; I slept.

I woke up four hours later, when I heard the announcement for Misato. I had a stinging headache from a jet lagged sleep.

Okay, in a few minutes, you have to see your wife.

Miya had had a month of her mother's cooking and cleaning and helping take care of the kids. All

I could do was hope that she was ready to see me again, and that she wouldn't be so angry.

That bullet train arrived at Misato Station 美郷駅 at 6:30 PM.

As the train door opened, I walked out onto the concrete station platform. The daytime heat of urban Tokyo had stripped away, and I was hit with the brisk fall northern Japanese air. I walked up that platform, stepped onto the escalator, and looked up at the sky to my left (east). It was a full moon. It glowed yellow and white, charging the Japanese sky.

I stared, totally zoned out for a second, trying to make sure that I was looking at the same moon I'd grown up with in Minnesota. I squinted. It looked alright.

I stepped off the escalator on the second floor, knowing my wife was about 100 yards away, close to me for the first time in a month.

I turned left (east), heading through the second-floor walkway, remembering my first trip to Misato –

Full Moon over Akita, Senshu Park, September 6th, 2017

My Son

5

*A*fter giving her that ring, Miya had told me that I should ask her parents for their daughter's hand, and that I should do it in person. We took that trip in December of 2002.

The Narita-to-Tokyo express train stopped at Tokyo Station. I stood up, and collected out luggage. Out of the corner of my eye, I saw Miya bolt out the door.

She waved me to her from the concrete platform.

"Come on. You're slow."

I shouted out to her in desperation, buried in our luggage.

"Where are we going?"

She crossed her arms, stomped her foot on the concrete, and darted left.

I dragged both our suitcases and threw one carry-on bag over either shoulder. I pushed past the crowd flooding into the train through the door I was attempting to exit, and escaped just as the door closed.

Miya was gone –

I was swept up in hundreds of people all turning left and heading down an escalator. When I got to the top of that escalator, I saw Miya getting off it at the bottom before turning left and disappearing.

I tried to keep up, dragging all our luggage onto two separate escalator stairs.

I caught a glimpse of her as the escalator cascaded down.

I shouted past the crowd.

"Where are we going?"

Bolting away, 100 feet from me, she looked back and shouted.

"You're slow!"

Then she disappeared down the white Tokyo Station hallway.

I got to the bottom of the escalator and tried to run through that white hallway.

After a few minutes of dragging all our luggage, I gave up. I stopped and dropped all four bags next to a giant white pillar.

I looked up.

How do they fit that much ceiling underground? That ceiling must be 30 feet high.

I looked left and right.

How can there be this many hallways?

All I saw were squiggles everywhere – no English.

I stacked all our luggage into a pile, sat on it, and crossed my arms, my back leaning against that pillar.

A few minutes later, Miya showed up.

"Where were you?" she said.

Wiping sweat from my forehead with my palm, I pointed at the sign above us:

秋田新幹線

➡

"Miya, what does that mean? It looks like the symbol on this piece of paper you gave me."

"I don't know" she said, "I'm not translator kind of person."

Then she charged away again, folding into the interweaving crowd of Tokyoites.

I picked up the two carry-on bags, slung them over my shoulders, and dragged the two luggage bags in her general direction.

A few minutes later, I saw her running back toward me again.

She shouted, pumping her fists toward the ground, her jet-black hair flailing.

"You are so slow!"

I dropped all the bags and shouted to her in the distance.

"Miya, are you just acting like you're going to ditch me here, or are you actually going to ditch me? I can't read any of these signs. I don't know where I am."

She marched to me and said, "You don't understand. We have to catch this train. They are never late."

I said, "We're catching a train?"

She squinted and nodded.

"Yes."

I said, "Why didn't you tell me?"

She said, "You don't even know where you are or how to do anything here."

I pointed at her luggage.

"Do you want to take one of these bags? I think maybe I can move a little faster if you take one of the bags."

She threw a carry-on over her shoulder, and ran down the hallway again.

I charged forward, on my own, into the crisscrossing crowd.

I next saw Miya 100 feet down the hall. She was flagging me down, telling me to meet her in front of a ticket gate.

When I got up to her she said, "Okay, we made it. We have an hour now. You are so slow. Let's go get some food."

I said, "What? We ran like that, and we have an hour?"

She took all the luggage and jammed it into some storage lockers, zapping some kind of card.

We went and sat on red stools at a random noodle shop.

I looked at the menu and found a series of squiggly lines.

"Miya, what kind of food do they have here?"

She stared at her menu.

"You can just order whatever you want."

I looked at the menu again, and flipped it over, showing it to her.

"I can't read this."

She looked at me from behind her menu.

"When I went to America, I had to do everything myself."

I tossed that menu on the table.

"Yes, but you're not by yourself. We're together."

She looked back down at her menu.

"You can never understand."

Silence.

She finally looked up at me again.

"You can even order chicken."

I smiled what felt like a very shitty smile.

"Okay, fine, I'll have some chicken."

Miya ordered... something.

The waitress brought me what looked like two deep fried ping pong balls on a leaf. Miya got a bowl of noodles, and a plate of... something.

I was trying really, really hard not to make a face.

"Miya, you know, you've got some squirming little white things on that plate."

When she put soy sauce on it, it squirmed even more, like it was convulsing.

I pointed at the plate.

"What is that?"

She looked down at the plate.

"It means it's fresh."

"Yeah," I said, "but what is it?"

She huffed and fluttered her eyes, avoiding eye contact.

"It's just normal food."

I pointed at it.

"I'm saying, what is *that*?"

She finally looked at me.

"It is what I ordered."

I leaned back and paddled the table.

"Okay. Never mind."

We caught the bullet train, riding for four-and-a-half hours in silence.

When we got to Miya's parents' home in Misato, her father Kentaro 賢太郎 (Ken-tah-row) met us at the front door. He looked deep into my eyes, shook my hand with both of his hands, and bowed.

Kentaro had white hair which flowed straight back, away from his sharp, angular features. He looked like a wise Native American chief, but in a gray pinstriped suit.

Miya dropped all her winter clothes at that front door and walked away.

I heard her voice echo down the hallway.

"Leave all those bags there. My mom will do it."

Miya's coat, hat, and gloves were collected off the floor by her mother.

Miya, already on her way up the staircase in front of us, shouted back, "That's my mom, Akiko 亜妃子 (Ah-key-ko)."

Akiko bowed to me with Miya's puffy winterwear bundled into her arms, then exclaimed, "Okaeri!"

before shuffling all Miya's stuff into the dark-stained wooden entryway closet on the left.

I flinched, and shouted to Miya, hoping she could hear me from wherever she had gone.

"Miya, what did your mom just say?"

Her shout echoed off the walls upstairs.

"She's welcoming you to her home! Bow to her!"

I bowed, flinching twice because I didn't know if I should bow or not, but I thought that I probably should. It was the first time that I had ever bowed, actually. Anyway, it wasn't a very good bow.

Miya ran down stairs and touched my right hand.

"Say *tah-dah-ima* ただいま."

I glanced at Miya.

"What does it mean?"

Miya looked back at me, her face lit up.

"It means you are home."

Akiko stood, smiling, waiting.

I bowed a better bow.

"Tadaima."

Akiko hugged me, then pushed me away at the shoulders.

She said, 「私の家が魚の臭いがしないことを願います。日本の家が外国人にとって魚の臭いがするという記事を読んだことがあります。あなたがここで心地が良い体験をするためにその臭いを消臭しようとしました。よろしくお願いします。」

Miya translated:

"I hope that my house doesn't smell like fish. I read that Japanese homes smell like fish to foreigners. I tried to eliminate the smell because I want you to enjoy your time here. Please be kind to me."

Akiko smiled and said some practiced English.

"You looks like strong American. My son."

Akiko bent in half at the waste, and stacked the two carry-on bags across her back. Then she whisked away all four bags, leaving her entryway a clean slate.

Kentaro & Akiko

賢太郎 亜妃子

Kentaro 賢太郎 was a salaryman for the national train company.

Kentaro had spent his youth living by himself in company-provided apartments all over Japan, working 60-to-80-hour weeks. Now in his late-50's, his schedule was still a series of oddly-timed naps followed by running back to the train station.

The first night I was there, I was up with jetlag when Kentaro woke up and left at 3:00 in the morning.

Akiko 亜妃子, later that afternoon, came home with a new purse. She called Miya into the first-floor bedroom.

From the hallway, I heard Akiko say, 「このバッグは私をお金持ちのような気分にさせてくれます。」

I walked into that room and found Akiko throwing this purse over her shoulder, and batting her eyes like Betty Boop.

I said, "Miya, what is she saying?"

Miya was staring at her mother in the mirror, her eyes big and flashing.

 "She's saying that the purse makes her feel *rich*."

I wrinkled my nose.

"Does it? How much did that purse cost?"

Miya was just locked in on her mother's image in the mirror.

"I don't know," she said, "Like, $2000 or something."

"Hmm," I said, "it should make her feel, like, $2000 more poor."

Miya snapped her head around and beamed her eyes through me like she might punch me, then she stomped away.

Every day, Akiko would put on an apron with blue and white and yellow checkers and duckies and flowers sewn into it. Then she would dart around the house cooking four-course meals, doing dishes, vacuuming, and doing laundry. When I woke up, she was doing housework. When I went to bed, she was still doing housework. She was like a live-in chef-maid.

I really did find her pretty annoying –

Akiko had never driven a car. She said she was afraid she wouldn't be able to find her way back home. That was annoying, but it was her doting on Miya that *really* bothered me.

"Miya, are you too hot? Miya, are you too cold? Miya, are you hungry?" she would say it while Miya chased her mother around the house like a personal assistant.

Akiko's endlessly asking Miya how she was, while Miya followed her around, taking orders – I found it odd. And the implication that, whatever was slightly wrong with Miya, her mother would immediately solve it – how could I ever compete with it?

Then there were Akiko's speeches, every word of which had to be translated *by Miya*, the subject of the speech.

As Kentaro drove us all to an onsen (hot spring) that weekend, I sat next to him in his Red Toyota. Miya and Akiko sat in the back.

Their location back there put this entire speech in stereo.

Akiko said, as though to nobody in particular, "Always remember that Miya is special and the most beautiful person around and buy her nice things and help her with the housework because I'm not there and you should always put her first and don't forget to support her in doing laundry and make sure she's always happy and unfold your socks so they're easy to wash and make sure you come back to Japan often and Miya is just so pretty – everybody says so – and don't do anything that makes her unhappy and don't drink too much or gamble and make sure you put your dishes on the counter..."

While she was in the middle of the speech, she had started looking in the rearview mirror, touching her hair, and batting her eyes at herself. Her hair was actually too short to change in any significant way by paying so much attention to it.

So, I had to listen attentively the first time, having no idea what she was saying, followed by listening to Miya prattle it all off again, for a second time, in English.

When Akiko started again, Miya shouted something I didn't understand. Then the car went silent.

I turned my head toward the back seat.

"Miya, what did you say?"

She leaned toward me.

"I told my mom to shut up."

I exhaled.

"Oh, thank God."

I came to find out later, when I learned some Japanese, that Miya had been interjecting her own opinions into her translations –

BACK TO

MINNESOTA

ミネソタ

I Wish I Was in Japan

6

*W*e continued to spend every weekend together until Miya graduated with that non-major degree in the spring of 2004.

I was making good money selling homes, and doing real estate seminars on the side. So, I bought a condo 15-miles west of Minneapolis, in Plymouth.

By the fall of 2005, we were married, and had our little one-year-old Kazuki. His little face was yellow, and his wispy black hair shot up all over the place.

We called him *Kazu-ducky* –

I'd rush home every day. I wanted to see them both as soon as I possibly could, and for as long as I could.

Miya would meet me at the door, bouncing.

"Tadaima!"

I would say, "okaeri."

And, holding our baby, she would kiss me all over my face.

She would cook a Japanese meal from scratch, then do all the dishes, and clean the house. She'd put Kazuki to bed, and we'd make love on the light-tan leather couch in the living room.

Then, Miya would whisper.

"I want to make sure you come back from work to a nice, clean home. I want to take care of you."

Life for the three of us was a cuddle-fest; hugs, and kisses, amazing foods, and wrapping ourselves up in big, puffy blankets.

And every time Miya tucked her hair behind her ear and smiled at me – with that *something* unspeakable in her eyes – she lit up my life.

Then, gradually, over the course of that winter, Miya turned quiet –

She would still always meet me at the door when I came home, but she didn't bounce around, she didn't kiss me anymore. She would just stand there in the doorway, holding our baby.

She would say "hi," with a blank look on her face, then turn away.

Sometimes, she would still cook. And, sometimes, she would still do the dishes, but not all the time. And, sometimes, after dinner, she would close herself and baby Kazuki into our bedroom, and they'd be gone for the night.

And, sometimes, she'd say, "I'm trying to do all housework, like my mom, but I can't do it. It's too hard. I'm not strong like my mom."

I would say, "I didn't marry your mom. I love you the way you are. We do things *together*."

Then... one cold, wet afternoon in March of 2006, I parked, and walked toward the main entrance of our condo building.

I looked to my right – past the melting ice, the wet pavement, and the muddy grass – and saw Miya's purple Honda StepWGN parked in front of our pale-yellow garage door.

Man, I hate that ugly-ass car.

Miya says it's good for her and the baby.

Stupid damn ugly car.

I opened the community door, walked 20 feet through the hallway, and opened the 1987-built door of our first-floor condo.

I stepped in, and found… nobody.

"Mi…. ya?" I said, turning and quietly shutting that old door behind myself.

I kicked off my shoes like I'd been trained to do, padlocked the door, then walked onto our light-tan carpet.

I looked across the living room.

"Miya.

"Miya, where are you guys?"

I marched past that tan leather couch on my right, down the carpeted hallway, and into the smaller bedroom. The room had no furniture, but I walked across the futon mat on the floor.

I pried open a space in the wooden shutters we'd installed together.

I looked past the windowpane we'd painted together.

Yup, her car is here. What the hell?

I shouted.

"Miya."

Silence -

Then I heard a groan in the other bedroom.

I bolted from that second room, went across the hall, and slid open the wooden white master bedroom door. I found Miya laying on the futon mat on the floor, curled up, facing the far wall.

She wasn't moving –

Baby Kazuki was rolling around on his back, next to her, next to the near wall. He looked up at me, kicking and wiggling and punching his little hands.

I kissed his little cheeks, and hugged him.

Miya's really not moving.

"Miya," I said.

"Miya, sweetheart, wake up."

I leaned over and shook her shoulder.

She inhaled.

"Miya... sweetie... what's the matter?"

She slowly rolled over, her face all puffy, and extended her index finger.

"You won't let me go outside."

I squinted.

"What?"

I looked down at our little Kazu-ducky, then back over at Miya.

She said, "You won't let me go outside."

She looked groggy. Her skin color was bad; yellow and green. She looked like she had the flu. Actually, she kind of looked like she was on drugs.

I said, "Miya, what? I love you. Come on. What are you talking about?"

I grabbed her by the hand and said, "Let me put Kazuki in the backpack, and let's go take a walk. It's beautiful out."

She retracted hand, rolling back toward the far wall.

"No. You won't let me."

Feeling spry, I jumped over her body and sat myself right in front of her.

"Come on Miya. Let's go take a walk."

She raised her head slightly.

"No... you won't let me."

I said, "Miya, what's the matter?"

She said, "You never help me do *anything*. And you *never* let me go outside."

I said, "I can help more around the house. You've been saying you want to do all the house stuff."

She said, "You don't take care of me. You don't help me with the baby. I'm trapped in here."

I rubbed her back.

"Okay. Okay. I'm just working all the time."

Miya dropped her head back to the futon mat.

I picked up little Kazuki, brought him to the living room, and popped in a DVD of Anpanman アンパンマン (a Japanese cartoon).

I went to the kitchen, and pulled out some food to cook dinner.

I shut the refrigerator door with my right foot, and Miya was right there – standing with her arms crossed.

I inhaled.

"Miya, you startled me. What are you doing?"

She peered into my eyes, those arms still crossed.

"I can't believe I changed my degree for you."

I said, "What?"

She said, "I changed my degree for *you*. That was so stupid. That was the worst mistake of my life."

I stepped away from her, put the pile of food on the counter, and pulled out a plastic white cutting board and a knife.

I put raw chicken and scallions on the plastic cutting board, and diced with my Chinese-made American knife.

"Miya, we've got little Kaz. We've got our home here in America. You don't have to live in Japan. I thought that's what you wanted when you got that student visa."

She squinted her eyes down small.

"I wish I was in Japan *right now*," she said, pointing at the wood-paneled floor.

I cut raw chicken with the smooth-edged blade.

"I love you. I love you so much, Miya. What's the matter?"

She looked at me with such a desperation in her eyes.

"Having a baby is too hard. I have to do *everything*. Usually, in Japan, we can get help from our mom."

I pulled a black pan from a lower counter, and a wooden spatula from the drawer, and put them on the counter.

I dropped my head, and chopped scallions.

"Miya, until the last few months, I thought we were doing really good – what is this?"

She drove her fists toward the floor so abruptly that I thought she might go right down with them.

"I wanna drink vinegar," she shouted, shaking her head.

My knife stopped moving, scallions on both sides of the blade.

I looked up at her.

"What?"

She stared through me, tears in her red eye.

She whispered, her voice trembling.

"I wanna drink vinegar."

So much pain on her face...

I placed the knife on the plastic white cutting board, and put my hands on the edge of the laminate white countertop.

I turned back to the living room –

Kazuki was rolling on the floor, sucking on his entire fist, drool dripping all over the carpet.

Anpanman pulled off his own head and fed it to a piece of bread with arms, legs, and a face.

I looked back to Miya, pushed my hands off the counter, and stood upright.

"Miya, what are we talking about right now?"

She said, "I wanna drink pickle juice. Is that pickle stuff calls juice or water?"

I shook my head.

"Miya, I don't know."

She said, "Why are you looking at me like that way? You think I'm crazy."

I said, "What? Why? No. I... I don't know. Miya — seriously — what are we talking about?"

She grabbed the wooden spatula I'd had sitting on the countertop next to me, and smashed it into the wood-paneled floor. It caromed off a kitchen cabinet.

She drove her fists toward the ground again.

"I'm *pregnant!*" she shouted, her black hair shaking wildly.

I looked at Kazuki again. He was still rolling around on the light-tan carpet, chewing his hand, watching Anpanman fly through the air.

I inhaled and, looked into Miya's beautiful brown eyes.

"Miya, are you really pregnant?"

She just stared at me.

So I pointed at the refrigerator.

"Do you want me to get you some pickles?"

She shook her head, trembling.

"I don't wanna have two kids in America. It's too hard. I need my mom's help."

I said, "Miya, I can help you."

She nodded, wiping tears from her eyes, her face trembling.

"I'm gonna go *home*," she said, "You can come too. We can live with my mom."

I grabbed her shoulders.

"Miya, our whole lives are here. We're gonna have a baby."

She rubbed tears around her face.

"You'll like it there," she said.

I said, "We have enough space here."

I embraced her, and pointed behind myself with my right thumb.

"We have our second bedroom."

Her face smashed into my chest, she said, "If we don't go to Japan, at least I wanna get a job, so I can feel some meaning to my life —"

Shattered

7

*B*y the fall of 2008, I would get up at around

7:30 – right as Miya would leave for work. I'd make breakfast, get the kids dressed, fed, and to preschool, work real estate, pick up the kids from preschool, cook dinner, bring the kids to Miya's office at 5:00, then continue onto Bloomington to teach real estate law from 6:00 to 10:00.

On this particular mid-September day, I woke up at 7:15, but laid in bed, listening to the wet leaves blustering on the trees, and Kazuki and Mae's little snores. It was the kind of day that seemed like it would be warm, but when you got out of the shower, that bitter Minnesota cold would prick all over your skin.

I was waiting for Miya to leave so that I wouldn't have to talk to her. I heard her mousing around, maybe making breakfast or something.

I had to go to the bathroom; I couldn't stand it. So, I got up. When I came out, I went to the kitchen to get something to drink.

Miya was sat at the kitchen table eating soba noodles. She looked toward me without looking directly at me.

"You never do the dishes," she said.

I looked over at her as I opened the refrigerator door, pulled out a can of sparkling water, and popped the tab.

"Huh? The dishes are clean. I loaded the dishwasher last night when I got home."

She stared straight ahead at the fireplace in the living room.

"You *never* do the dishes."

I put the can on the white kitchen counter.

"Okay, so I'll do the dishes right now."

I began unloading the dishwasher.

She glared at me.

"That dishwasher is just crap. You have to buy a new one."

I pulled out a clean glass, closed the dishwasher door, and leaned against the counter. I picked up the can, poured the sparkling water into the glass, took a drink, and put the glass down on the white laminate kitchen counter.

"I don't know if we can afford that right now," I said.

She squinted.

"That's because you are not willing to work."

I shook my head.

"Do you know how nuts this stuff is? Seriously, I'm doing the dishes right now. I'm going to work right now, right after you leave."

She stared out the double-pane sliding glass door.

"It's not enough. You don't make enough money."

I said, "Okay, do you understand that the economy of the entire planet is falling apart? I work with real estate and mortgages. Both markets are ruined. The financial markets are ruined. Banks are failing. You should be happy we both have jobs."

Miya got up, walked over to me, took the glass from the counter, and smashed it into the hardwood kitchen floor. It shattered into a thousand pieces.

She screamed, driving her fists toward the floor.

"*You* are nuts! You are! That's not real job! It's not even hard! You don't have a job because you are too *stupid* to do anything."

She ran and bolted through the front door, slamming it so hard that it shook the wall, jostling our framed family pictures.

I looked down at the broken shards of glass all around my feet, then walked over to the calendar on the wall next to the fridge. I hoped to see a date with no work, so that I could make a run for Canada with the kids. I couldn't find one.

Just then, I heard somebody lumbering.

I peeked my head around the corner and found four-year-old Kazuki slowly crawling down the hallway as though he were a baby.

"Hey, Kazuki?" I said.

He pushed himself off his hands and knees and came running down the hall to me.

He crashed into my legs.

"Daddy, you and momma are loud."

I got on my knee and crushed his little body to mine.

"I know sweetheart. I'm so sorry. I just don't know what to do anymore –"

Family Picture

8

*T*he following morning, I woke up at 7:30

when I heard Miya unlock the front door.

I pounced out of bed, down the light tan carpeted hallway, and turned right – to the front entry.

"Miya," I said.

She looked at me with a smile.

"Huh? You wanna kiss me goodbye?"

I leaned in and kissed her on the cheek.

"Miya," I said, "I had to clean up all that glass yesterday."

She touched my face.

"You did good. The house is so clean. I really appreciate it."

I winced.

"You do?"

"Yeah," she said, then leaned in and kissed me, drawing her hand across my cheek.

"I'm sorry," she said, "I'll never do like that again."

I nodded.

"Okay."

She said, "My company is sending me to research some technology stuff at the Tokyo Motor Show. You and the kids can come with. My mom said she'll watch the kids. Do you have something you want to do in Japan at that time?"

My eyes lit up.

"Yeah, I want to go climb the mountains in Nagano."

She patted my face.

"Okay, good. I made you and the kids breakfast. It's on the counter. I hope you like it."

I leaned in and kissed her neck, then rubbed my face against her cheek, mumbling.

"Thank you. I love you."

She stuck out her lips for me to kiss her.

"I have to go," she said, "I'll wait up for you tonight so we can cuddle on the couch."

I nodded.

"Okay."

She said, "And I booked someone to take more family pictures this weekend. This time of year – it will be so beautiful. And the kids are so cute."

She tucked her hair behind her ear, flashed her smile, and walked out the door. I gently shut it.

I turned around and found two tiny children climbing on our tan leather couch in their pajamas.

"Daddy!" they shouted, bouncing around.

As we sat and ate the eggs and noodles Miya had cooked, the black cordless phone on the white kitchen counter rang.

"Hello," I said, sitting next to the kids at the kitchen table.

My older brother Eric said, "Hey."

I said, "Hey."

He said, "Well… you sound pretty good."

I said, "Yeah, I'm great! Why?"

He said, "Mom said Miya was throwing stuff around the house again."

I said, "No – I mean – that was a long time ago. We're doing great. Actually, we're going to the Tokyo Motor show, and I'm gonna go climb some mountains. I can't wait."

He paused, then said, "Well... that was *yesterday*. Mom said you were trying to figure out if you had to take the kids and go stay with her."

I shook my head, and stuck my tongue out at Mae.

"No. I don't want to leave Miya by herself. We're doing great, and we're doing family pictures this weekend."

He said, "Okay... well... Mom just asked me to check in on you."

I said, "Alright, well, I don't wanna talk about any bad stuff, okay? Everything's great. We're doing family stuff right now, and Miya's happy. She's so excited we're going to Tokyo. I can't wait."

He exhaled.

"Hm. Ok-*ay*?"

I said, "Okay. Bye."

He said, "Bye –"

MISATO

美郷

Go Home and Die

9

*I*n November 1st of 2011 at 6:30 PM, I looked up

at the full moon hanging in the rural Misato sky, walked across the train platform, and stepped onto the escalator. At the top, I showed my train ticket to a man in a blue uniform, and turned left, walking into Misato Station 美郷駅. The walkway was covered by a towering thirty-foot ceiling.

I darted past a second-floor noodle shop and a convenience store – anxious to see Kazuki and Mae as fast as I could. I hurried toward the elevator five hundred feet in front of me, as I tried to visualize how Miya might behave when I saw her.

Having crossed over the tracks, I got in that elevator, dragging my luggage bag behind me. The door opened into the street, and I walked back out into the cool evening.

To my right was a circular driveway loaded with yellow and white taxis. To my left was a multi-colored bus picking up people. And right in front of me, on the sidewalk, was my beautiful – pissed-off-looking – wife in a cute puffy red coat.

Her shiny black hair bounced off her shoulders. She hadn't aged a minute from the day I'd met her.

I said, "Hi."

She glanced at me.

"How was your trip?"

I glanced at her, then walked to the trunk of the car.

"Fine. I'm tired. Tokyo is hard work."

She winced.

"Hmph. You look homeless. You have to shave your beard."

She got in her dad's red Toyota four-door, and popped the trunk. I threw in my luggage, and got in the left passenger-side seat.

We pulled away, past the taxis and buses.

I produced a smile through my headache.

"It's nice to see you."

She didn't look at me.

"Yeah."

Uncomfortable, I laughed.

"It's good to be speaking English."

Silence.

All I could hear was the engine humming and the tires hitting the road.

"Miya, where are the kids?"

"They're at home," she said.

I raised my eyebrows.

"Why didn't they come with?"

She blinked several times.

"I didn't want to bother them. They are playing."

I pressed my eyebrows down.

"Hm, like, do they know I'm coming?"

She flashed her eyes toward me, blinking, keeping her attention to the road.

"I think so."

The engine whirred against silence.

"Miya," I said, burning inside for some hint of warmth, "I actually feel a little sick. Tokyo; that city was hard by myself."

In my mind, my loving wife said, *You're okay, baby. We're just happy you're finally here. I love you so much. I missed you.*

In my mind, she pulled over, passionately kissed me, and said, *You'll be healthy in no time my sweet man. You are young and you are strong. You just need some rest. You're gonna be great tomorrow.*

Instead, she pulled into her parent's driveway, and stared at me.

"The kids are doing really good here and they don't need you to tell them that you are sick and weak."

I shook my head.

"I'm just telling you – I've got a headache. I think it's jetlag."

She threw the car into park.

She said, "So why don't you go home and *die?*"

She bolted from the car and into the house.

I just sat there. I never did answer. I was pretty sure that it was a rhetorical question –

Akiko's Turf

亜妃子の区域 10

So, on November 1st of 2011, I stepped through the front door and into Akiko's home at 7:00 PM.

I dropped my luggage in the doorway, where I saw nobody.

I said with a smile, "Tadaima."

Silence.

I kicked off my shoes, stepped through the entryway, and turned to the kitchen to my right.

Sitting at her kitchen table twenty feet away, Akiko flashed her eyes at me, then rolled them, making a disgusted noise.

"Hmph."

Then she looked back to the TV on the kitchen counter.

I looked around, hoping that Kentaro would show up, so that I could see a kind face.

I tossed my bright blue carry-on bag on a stand-alone counter next to the kitchen table, then ran down the dark-stained wood-paneled hallway to the first-floor bedroom – to my children.

Kazuki & Mae

和樹　鳴

Kazuki was born on December 8th of 2004.

He was missing one of his front teeth, and his black hair shot straight back, like his grandpa, Kentaro's. He looked like a little Hawaiian version of me.

Mae was born on December 8th of 2006.

Mae (May) was missing all four of her front teeth. She had lily white skin and light brown hair. She had light-brown eyes and her mother's high cheekbones. She looked like a little Caucasian version of her Momma.

When I entered the room, Kazuki was pounding his mini taiko drum 太鼓 and Mae was making some manga 漫画 drawings.

They looked up and screamed, running and smashing into my legs.

"Daddy!!"

I crouched down and wrapped my arms around them.

"Hi guys!"

They screamed.

"Hi!"

Mae patted my black beard.

"Daddy…"

"Yes Peanut," I said, as she shoved her hand in my mouth.

She tried to pry my mouth open and look in it like I was an alligator or something.

"Where were you?" she said.

I pulled her hand out of my mouth and said, "Yuck, Mae."

She threw her head back.

I grabbed her little cheeks, and hugged her.

"I was in America! How are you?"

She shouted.

"Good!"

Mae rubbed her hand on the top of my head, scrambling up my hair.

"Daddy – ?" she said.

I looked into her light brown eyes.

"Yes, Peanut?"

She grabbed my face with both hands.

"When are we gonna go see Gwamah and Gwumpa?"

I tried to talk as she smooshed my face and gave me fish lips.

"Don't wowwy, Peanut, we'w go see dem in deh spwing."

She shouted back, nearly bursting my eardrums.

"OH-Kay! –"

I popped my eyes wide open and retracted my head.

We ran around, screaming and wrestling.

A few minutes later, Miya 美哉 came stomping her feet down that wood-planked hallway where she found me laying on the floor – Kazuki and Mae sitting on my back.

Miya stopped, posing in the doorway, holding her closed gray laptop.

I looked up at her from the tatami mat-covered floor as the kids bounced on my back.

"What is it?" I said.

She shook the laptop at me.

"Where's my computer power cord?"

I flipped over as the kids wiped out on the floor.

"What?" I said.

She shouted.

"Where's my cord? I had it... and *you* took it!"

I put my hands up as I rolled over on my back on the tan tatami mat floor.

"I just got here. Why would I have your computer thing?"

She shouted.

"Don't touch my stuff!"

She bolted back down the hallway.

I got up and walked into the living room near the front of the house, right next to the kitchen, with Mae wrapped around my leg and Kazuki chasing me and punching me in the butt.

I found Miya sitting on the couch, her eyes squinted down, her arms crossed over her computer in front of her.

Mae began peeling stickers off a sheet of paper and sticking them all over my pants.

"Okay," I said to Miya, "let's just look for it. Where did you have it last?"

She looked up at me for a split second, then back at the TV.

"You can never touch my stuff. That's mine."

She took her laptop off her lap, stood up next to me, and tossed the computer into the light brown leather living room couch where she'd been sitting. Then she stormed away, pounding her feet up the stairs, and slamming the second-floor bedroom door behind herself —

Kazuki's Passport

11

*I*n the weeks leading up to Kazuki's birth in the

fall of 2004, I had sat down next to Miya, trying to get her help in naming him.

It was a wet and cold autumn Friday, the kind of Minnesota night where the misty rain would turn to snow, and where high school kids would play football under hazy lights.

Miya was wearing a black slip, covered in a big, puffy blanket, laying on the light tan leather couch in our Plymouth condo living room.

Holding some folded-up pieces of paper, I sat at her feet.

"Miya, do you like any of these names?"

She muttered.

"I don't wanna think about it. Just pick one."

I pointed at the hand-written list of names.

"Don't you have some idea about it?"

She curled up, facing the couch, then she looked back toward me.

"I want it to be Japanese."

I sat up straight, put on my glasses, and shuffled through my hand-written papers.

"Okay, I have a list of Japanese names. What about *Kazuki*? I like that one. Do you like that one?"

She buried her face back into the couch.

"I don't know. I guess so."

I dropped the paper on the coffee table.

"Well, I like it. What's the proper spelling?"

She sat up.

"So, give me a pen."

She wrote:

和樹

Then she laid back down.

I sat beside her on that tan leather couch, in my checkered pajama pants and white t-shirt.

"Whoa, that's cool. How do I write that in English?"

She slightly looked toward me again.

"I don't know. Just – you decide."

Having tried for half a year to have this conversation, this was the furthest I'd ever got. So, I tried to take it as far as I could.

"Okay, but I've seen two spellings for that. I've seen it with a z and with an s."

She said, "I don't know that kind of stuff. That's American stuff."

I said, "Okay, but... we have to figure out how to spell it in English."

She rolled over and stuffed her face back into the couch.

"Can you just shut up? You're bothering me."

The following evening, I tried again as we lay in bed.

"Miya, what do you think of that name – Kazuki?"

She exhaled loudly.

"We already had that conversation. Why do you want to talk about it again? It's done. Don't you remember?"

So, after our son's birth, the nurse asked me to write his name for the birth certificate. I had to try one more time, and if it had to be as she lay in her hospital bed, that's what it would have to be.

"Miya, do you want me to spell little Kaz's name with an s or with a z?"

"It doesn't matter," she said, "I'll register it the right way in Japan."

I showed her the document the nurse had just given me.

"I'm saying – for his birth certificate, in America – I need his name spelling."

She patted my hand.

"I'll do it in Japan. It's fine."

I pointed at the line I had to fill out.

"Okay, Miya, how do you want me to spell his name on his birth certificate – this American birth certificate – right here?"

Her face closed down as she whispered in staccato.

"I. don't. wanna. think about it. I. just. had. a baby. It's American stuff. You supposed to do it."

Then she rolled over on her side, and stared out the open window at the winter sun shining off the snow.

So, I left, and went down the hall to visit Kas/zuki.

I looked at our tiny little baby swaddled in that blue blanket in that clear plastic crib, and shook my head.

I looked down at the document and made an executive decision –

Kasuki.

When little *Kasuki* was three years old, we enrolled him in a Japanese school in Minneapolis which ran on Sundays.

As Miya and I sat at a table at the school, the Japanese woman enrolling him looked at me like I'd just told her a pretty good joke.

"Why did you spell his name that way?"

I raised my eyebrows, glancing at Miya for a second.

"How did you know that I was the one who spelled it that way?"

The woman cupped her hand over her mouth and snickered.

"Because Japanese people don't spell this name that way."

I looked over at Miya again. She kept her eyes on the woman, and the two began speaking in Japanese.

Driving the silver Saturn Vue back home, with three-year-old Kasuki and one-year-old Mae in their car seats, I turned to Miya.

"Why did you have me spell his name that way?"

She looked at me with a scowl.

"I didn't do that. That's American stuff. *You* did it."

I said, "Well don't you think we should fix it?"

She said, "You are only putting the heater on yourself. I am so disappointed. You are supposed to think about your kids more than you."

I paused for a moment, then pointed my fingers up as my palms rested on the steering wheel.

"The heaters are on everybody. This truck has, like, eight heaters."

Silence.

In October of 2011, with *Kasuki's* passport ready to expire in December of 2011, and with our leaving the U.S. for several months – Miya and I went to the courthouse and had his name changed to *Kazuki*. Then I ordered him a corresponding new U.S. passport, which I would then bring with me to Japan.

None of this had been a problem for his travel on October 3rd of 2011. As far as Japan was concerned, his name had always been 和樹. And Japanese citizen 和樹 had left the U.S. and entered Japan on his Japanese passport.

So – when I had come to Japan, I had come with Kazuki's new U.S. passport stuffed into my bright blue carry-on bag. And I had just dumped that blue bag containing Kazuki's passport on Akiko's kitchen table in Misato.

The next day, November 2nd, I woke up and rambled down Akiko's ¾-sized staircase to find that the bright blue bag I'd left on the counter was now unzipped and tipped over sideways. I dug through it and found that my wallet, jacket, travel pillow, and passport were all there, but Kazuki's new U.S. passport was gone.

Miya was cooking breakfast with her mother.

I stood next to my blue bag.

"Miya, where's Kaz's passport?"

She didn't look at me, steam rising from the pan, as she threw in diced scallions.

"Huh?"

I said, "Where's his passport that I brought from Minnesota?"

"Oh," she said, continuing to cook, "It's gone."

I continued to look at the back of her head, hoping for eye contact, but getting none.

"I know it's gone. Where is it?"

She tossed diced chicken and scallions with long chop sticks.

"It's in a safe place," she said.

It occurred to me – all at once – that I had spent so much time and energy trying to figure out the implications that Miya could easily replace their Japanese passports in the U.S., that I had absolutely *no idea* the implications if I had to replace *their U.S. passports in Japan*.

All I could think of was that, whenever we had come back from Japan, we had handed both the U.S. and Japanese passports to... people. Airline people? Customs people? I didn't know who actually needed what or why.

Miya had got Kazuki out of America and into Japan with only his Japanese passport. *Was one passport enough to get him out?*

What would it actually take to get the kids out of this country if she reneged on our agreement?

I stood in the seemingly-insulation-free hallway between the living room and the steaming kitchen. My cold, bare feet gripped the slippery wood-planked floor.

"Miya, listen, you can't do this. Where are the kids' passports?"

She slammed her long set of wooden cooking chopsticks on the counter and marched over to me.

"I'm so done with America! I'm never going back there again!"

I drove my index finger at the floor.

"You said you were coming here no matter what, and this could even be a trip!"

She pointed her index finger to the floor.

"This is *not* a trip! The kids are doing so good in school. I don't take them out! You have to think of what's best for kids! Don't be selfish!"

I raised my eyebrows and pointed my thumb to the bedroom where the kids were playing.

"As soon as Mae saw me, she asked me about going to see Grandma and Grandpa in Minnesota."

Miya dropped her voice.

"She's little. Mae doesn't know anything about this kind of stuff."

I squinted in disgust.

"About what kind of stuff? *Lying about what you're really going to do* kind of stuff?"

She crossed her arms.

"You just want to fight."

She stormed back to the kitchen.

I followed her.

"No, I don't want to fight. I want to know where their passports are."

She locked her eye contact to the chicken and scallions she was cooking, picking up those long wooden chopsticks.

"You have to show me you can work on it. Getting mad at me does you no good *at all*. I should divorce you right now, just like everybody around me says."

I looked behind myself, as though I might find somebody else to talk to, then looked back at her.

"I just got here. I'm just saying, *where is his passport?*"

She slammed the long wooden chop sticks down into the counter a second time, sending little pieces of chicken and scallion ricocheting.

"Being mad at me cannot help you – at all – *here*. You *always* took advantage of me before. I was the one who was so subordinate."

She stuck her finger in my face.

"Now I can do it *to you!* You are ME now! SO subordinate! I'll give that back once I'm done with ALL legal stuff."

I said, "What legal stuff?"

She scowled.

"You will find out so soon. I already started that action at the government office before you came here —"

Get a Job

12

It was my second evening on Akiko's Turf 亜妃子

の区域, and the kids were upstairs getting ready
for bed. Miya 美哉 and her mother were in the
main-floor bedroom. Then, their chatting turned
into a battle.

This fight probably meant that Miya would spend
the next couple of days talking to me about all
the things that made Akiko a bad person, instead
of talking to me about all the things that made
me a bad person – *which was great*.

I heard Akiko from down the hall, in the first-floor
bedroom.

「あなたの夫は仕事もたない です 。」

Miya hollered back.

「君は何知らない。黙れ！」

Their arguing escalated as I slinked my way down
the hall, past the front entry, and toward that
bedroom.

I peeked my head out from behind the doorway and saw a clean and open floor, covered in tan (rush-covered straw) tatami mats. The room was vacant of furniture – nothing but Kazuki's new black electric piano, a few of Mae's drawings stuck to the walls, and the closet built into the left wall.

The tan room looked like everything had been cleared away for a Japanese brawl, and the two were facing off right in the middle.

Akiko – shorter than short-Miya – got up in her daughter's face. Miya 美哉 pointed back as the two jawed.

Akiko 亜妃子 slapped her daughter across the head, striking her right temple with her open left hand.

Miya grabbed her mother by the shoulders and shoved her to the ground with a guttural scream.

Akiko, in her checkered ducky apron, got up and resumed arguing.

I stood in the hallway, right outside the doorway, stupefied.

Just then, I felt someone behind me.

My little boy was standing at the top of the stairs. He was blankly staring at it all, like it was the sumo tournaments he would watch on TV. I ran upstairs, grabbed him, and brought him to bed.

The next day, I asked Miya – as she rushed around the kitchen – why they'd been arguing.

She responded flippantly, as she ran around preparing a meal.

"My mom was saying you supposed to get a job right away. She said men are not supposed to be at home."

I place the pads of my fingers and thumb onto the kitchen countertop.

"I just got here."

She glanced toward me, before cutting carrots with her mother's Japanese blade.

"I don't know. That's Japanese culture stuff. That's like... shame stuff."

I patted the counter.

"Well... it's ridiculous. I just got here."

Miya said, "She's thinking you were just always working such easy stuff in America. She's saying you have to get ready to work harder. Japanese work harder."

I grabbed her by the arm, and spun her around to face me.

I pulled her to me.

"Miya, what about us spending some time together?"

She stared at me.

"Japanese cannot think like that way."

I said, "I'm asking *you* to think that way. I haven't seen you in a month."

So, Miya and I went out to dinner that night. And Miya did, in fact, complain to me about her mother.

I was happy to be the good guy for a minute… more like relieved –

Reality Raining Down

13

*I*shot up off the futon mat and looked around.

I'd been dreaming of blasting through green forests on the bullet train. I grabbed my head, but the wavering persisted. I wondered for a moment if it was an earthquake – it wasn't. It was in my head.

I tried to tame my racing mind as it burst through scene-after-scene on that bullet train.

Okay, I'm sitting on a bed on the floor. I'm on the other side of the planet. I'm not traveling. I'm not in Tokyo. I'm here.

Rain thudded off the walls, as though off an old tent, and it *pinged* off the metal roof.

In the corner, there were three blankets stacked on three futons. I tossed off a blanket, crawled off that futon – the only bedding which had not been swept off the tatami mat floor – and went to the window.

The clock on the counter read *7:42.*

"Anybody here?"

I almost shouted it. Then I turned from the window, hearing it ring through the hallway and down the staircase.

I was trying, hard, to accept that this place was real; my reality. It was not working. It was like I was living it and also watching myself live it. It made me want to do more than just pinch myself; I kind of wanted to punch my own brains out.

I looked out that window as gray clouds poured down on the neighborhood.

I looked at the electrical wires interweaving above the street.

I looked at the neighbors' ¾-sized houses built within a few feet on either side.

I looked below. There was no garage, but the rain was pounding off the steel-framed car port sheltering Kentaro's red Toyota.

I looked out that window as far as I could see, at the gray mist rising from the distant mountains. A feeling of empty nothingness washed over me.

I walked out of the bedroom, ducking slightly through the ¾-height doorway, down the ¾-sized stairs, and past the ¾ wide walls covered with pale yellow wallpaper.

Believing – but not positive – that I was alone, I shuffled through the kitchen drawers for Kazuki's passport. I checked in-and-around that wooden counter next to the kitchen where I'd left my blue bag a few days earlier – no passport.

I looked, the rain pelting loudly off the metal roof and the thin walls, at the shrine between the kitchen and the living room.

There was incense in a clay jar, two little statues of Buddha, and some message on parchment paper – I couldn't read it.

And there was a picture of Akiko's parents. They had gone to war with my country in 1941. My grandfather-in-law had lost his eye as a pilot during that war. Miya didn't know how; he had never talked about it.

I wondered if he had bombed Pearl Harbor on the same date as Kazuki and Mae's birthday – Japan's December 8th.

Standing in front of that shrine, I smelled vegetables and fish and grass and ozone coming in from all around. I smelled the unfinished wood that framed the house.

With no central air, the temperature inside had dropped to match the rain-chilled outside air, and I felt the cold against my arms.

Suddenly the almost-black wooden front door swung open and Akiko and my children poured into the house with noise, umbrellas, and raincoats.

Kazuki yelled.

"Shut up Mae!"

Mae shouted back.

"No, YOU shut up, stupid!"

Kazuki retorted.

"No, YOU'RE stupid!"

Mae punched Kazuki in the back of the head and he flopped on the floor in front of the door he'd just entered. The five-year-old brute just stood there, staring at him.

Kazuki flopped around like a fish. Then he began crying – more like complaining. He was flopping around, pounding on the floor, and complaining.

I darted over to them, my parental instinct stronger than my trepidation over the fact that Akiko was standing right there.

"Hey, you *guys* – Mae, don't hit your –"

Akiko stepped in front of me, and scolded my children.

「喧嘩はやめろ。お母さんが帰って来た時に怒られるぞ。」

She talked right over my talking, which she couldn't understand any more than I could understand hers.

I tried again.

"Hey, guys –"

Akiko 亜妃子 continued to scold.

「君たちは兄妹だ。おたがい優しくしなさい。じゃないと後でひどい目にあうからね。」

I put my hand up like a traffic cop in front of Akiko.

"Excuse me. Please give me a minute to talk to my children."

She said it in English.

"Kazuki, you can't cry! No cry! Bad!"

Trying to get her to look at me, I tapped my chest.

"I will talk to my kids about this."

She laughed, storming toward her kitchen, and said, 「Hmph. *Gaijin* 外人。」

My mother-in-law had just called me the slang term for *foreigner*. A more direct translation would be *outsider*.

I went upstairs and looked out the window again at the gray sky and the pounding rain. My heart pounded so fast. That rain pounded so heavy.

I have to get out of this fucking house –

A few moments later, Miya showed up and told the kids to get ready for school.

I darted over to meet her in the entryway.

"Where were you?"

She walked past me, and into the kitchen.

"We needed groceries."

At 8:00, Miya left to bring the kids to school.

I got on my computer and did a search:

American citizen support in Japan

I found that Misato was in the jurisdiction of the U.S. Consulate of Sapporo.

I wrote down the phone number and headed outside.

Underneath that carport, I found Akiko's bike. It was white, with a rusty frame of two curvy steel rods. It had a bell and a Wicked Witch of the West basket. I took it and went out into the rain, looking for a payphone.

I peddled a few blocks east, away from the train station and toward the mountains. I stopped at a red light and looked around at all the signs that I couldn't read. They were drenched in rain water. They looked so cold.

I turned to my right and headed south, peddling a woman's bike in the pounding rain in northern Japan, completely isolated from everybody who loved and supported me.

After a few miles of peddling, I saw a big mall at the top of a hill. The pink sign out front said *Aeon*.

I pulled up to the mall, parked in the ramp, and pumped yen-after-yen into a green payphone I found on the wall. All the buttons were in Japanese and the recorded message was in Japanese. After pumping $20-worth of yen into the machine, I finally got the consulate's voicemail; they were closed.

I gave up, went back out into the pounding rain, got my mother-in-law's bike – with its big basket – and headed back down the hill.

That evening, sitting at the kitchen table, I tried again.

"Hey Miya, I was just going to put my passport away. I'm thinking to put it with the kids' passports. Where are those?"

She looked slightly my direction, from under her eyebrows, while cooking dinner with her mother, then looked back down at the pan.

"They're gone. They're in a safe place. I already told you."

I looked right at her as she refused to reciprocate eye contact.

"So, where should I put my passport?"

"I don't know," she said, continuing to cook, "That's not my problem. Just put it wherever you want. Why don't you stop thinking about it, and try to find a job?"

I went upstairs to the bedroom, sat in the pile of futon bedding which had been spread across the floor, and did a search for *Sapporo* 札幌.

I found that Misato's jurisdiction for American citizen support was on Hokkaido 北海道, Japan's northern island, and that it was six hours away by bus, then airplane, then bus, or twelve hours away by overnight ferry or underwater train.

A week later, I landed a job in Niseko ニセコ, Hokkaido, which would start on December 1st. I would be an English teacher at a Japanese kindergarten in a rural ski resort town. More importantly, I would be two-hour's drive from the U.S. Consulate of Sapporo.

My new boss, a New Zealander named Jude, called and asked me to have my wife help setup an account at the Misato post office. They would direct deposit my salary into that account.

I drove Miya, in her father's red Toyota, to the post office about three miles west of the house.

When we got there, the post office employee pointed at me, making no eye contact with me, and talked to Miya.

「あなたは外国人で日本に六か月間住んでいないことから、郵便アカウントを作ることはできません。」

Miya translated.

"Since you are a gaijin 外人, and you have not been living in Japan for six months, you cannot open an account."

I smacked open the steel-framed glass door, and stormed outside.

Standing on the concrete sidewalk, I yelled.

"This is discrimination. This is crazy."

Miya followed me outside and screamed.

"This is *exactly* like when I had to open my account in Saint Cloud! That was so hard! I even had people yelling at me!!"

I screamed back.

"You couldn't open an account in Minnesota because you were a foreigner? That did not happen! What are you talking about?"

She screamed back.

"I had to do *all* this by *myself* when I was in Minnesota! I didn't have help from anybody!"

She extended her hand.

"Give me the car key!"

Since it was her father's car, I gave her the key.

She stomped to the car, got in, and drove away.

I called my boss, Jude, and told him I couldn't open an account because I was a foreigner.

He said, "That's fucking bullshit! I'll take care of it. Give the phone to that racist fucking asshole."

I put the guy on the phone with Jude.

I don't know what they said to each other, but I got an account, and was handed a passbook and a passbook (account access) card.

I walked the three miles back to the house.

Miya 美哉 came to me in the entryway.

"I'm not going to help you with *anything* anymore. And you can't drive my dad's car. You're gonna break it."

I walked right past her, to the foot of the stairs.

"I opened the account. Jude helped me."

She stomped, as loudly as she could, to the kitchen.

I went upstairs and put the account documents in my blue bag in the bedroom.

The next morning, I woke up – alone on the futon on the floor – and started packing to go up to Hokkaido. I started packing my blue bag and found that my account passbook was still there, but my account access card was gone.

My stomach sank, then churned into a knot. I felt a tingle down my arms.

I went down to the kitchen, where Miya was cooking breakfast with her mother.

"Miya, where is my passbook card?"

She didn't look at me.

"Your what?"

I stepped in front of her so that she would see me even if she didn't look.

"My passbook card. I have my passbook, but the account access card is missing."

She glanced over – looking me up and down as though I was begging for change. Then she looked back down at her sizzling food.

"Oh, I need that."

I crossed my arms.

"Where is it?"

She looked me in the eye, then looked away.

"It's in a safe place."

I inhaled, then exhaled.

"Where is it?"

She raised her eyebrows, still looking down.

"I need that."

So, between Miya and her mother, I was being intermittently ignored, laughed at, called racial slurs, and yelled at. Miya had revoked my right to drive the family car, she had gone from threatening to abandon me in Japan to actually abandoning me. She had both the kids' passports, and now she had access to the only account I was going to be able to open.

Miya had effectively taken control of every single thing.

I had been in Japan for eight days…

HOKKAIDO

北海道

Lost in Hokkaido

海道 14

*O*n November 27th, I took the world's longest

under-ocean train. It shot north to Aomori – the northern tip of the island of Honshu – before diving into a black cave, as though bolting through a mine shaft. The train reemerged an hour later, with a blast of harsh winter sunlight and snow and mountains, on the northern island of Hokkaido. The train continued north and east until it stopped at Sapporo Station at 8:30 AM.

After walking around the station for a few minutes, I found the east exit. I made my way outside, and stepped onto the concrete city sidewalk, as puffy snow fell from the gray-washed sky.

My new boss, Jude, picked me up in a white van –

I was alarmed at Jude's tall, skinny stature and his brown hair shaved almost bald. He looked to me like an extremist of some kind – with his hawk-like eyes and that gaunt, angular face – but he was in a suit and tie. Despite the suit, the word *skinhead* came to mind.

His Kiwi accent was thick.

"Ay mate, 'ow was youwa travels?"

My head was spinning an unspeakable kind of anxiety.

"Um… good."

"No troubles?" he said.

I exhaled.

Am I about to actually have a real conversation with someone in this country?

"Well," I said, "it's pretty hard to figure out directions in those big train stations, isn't it? I wasn't sure which exit you'd be at. That station is huge."

He snapped his head and looked at me cross as he pulled the van into traffic.

"If youwa gonna live in their country, you'd betta learn theya bloody fucking language, don't you think? You coudn't even open youwa own bloody account."

I shook my head and blinked a few times, startled, then smiled and laughed in discomfort.

"Isn't that kind of hard, learning to read Japanese? I've only been here for three weeks."

He glared at me with a raised eyebrow, then peered back through the windshield, weaving through Sapporo's city traffic.

"It's just a bloody fucking excuse, idn't it? Just anotha fucking lazy American, raw-ight?"

He nodded at me as though I was required to nod back.

I looked away from him, out the windshield at the icy road, with a defiant scoff.

"*Right*."

I glanced at him again, as we caromed down the city street. Jude had a scar over his left eyebrow.

After two days of training in Sapporo, Jude walked me back to that white van, now parked in front of the company's downtown office building. There, he introduced me to an exhausted-looking salaryman in a gray, pinstriped suit.

The stout man entered the right side, gesturing for me to walk around. I entered the left, passenger-side of that tiny white roller skate van, under a high blue sky and a white sun.

The door crunched with the sound of icy friction when it opened, and then again when it closed. Once inside, the van went silent.

The man cranked his bundle of keys, and the van fired up. Only the engine's rumbling, the blasting heater, and a Japanese talk radio show ran in the background.

The woman on the radio, giggling in her low-pitched voice, bouncing off the cold van walls, further creeped me out –

This man glanced at me once as he pulled out, and weaved through city traffic, then into the mountainous countryside.

As the city stripped away to brown forest covered in snow drifts twice the height of the car, I looked at this man.

"It's cold here," I said.

He pointed out the windshield with his white-gloved hand.

"Japanese snow."

Then, he nodded.

Total silence —

Those were the last words spoken between us for the next two-and-a-half hours.

As the expressway above the city jogged left, to the southwest, he began to play with his phone and shuffle through a pile of disorganized documents. Then he began to actually read them as he drove through the blustering rural snow.

Is he pretending he can't see me because I'm white? Because I don't speak Japanese? Because of some cultural thing?

After two-and-a-half hours of scrolling past snow-covered forest in total silence — aside from a woman's eerie talk radio show gnawing at my brain, and this stranger mumbling to himself while driving — we arrived.

Niseko was a small town dwarfed by mountains on every side.

As we pulled into the school district office, the 4:30 PM sun was setting.

In front of me was a towering Mount Fuji-lookin' thing. It had its own white cloud for a hat.

I wonder if that mountain would have a normal conversation with me in English...

Man... I must really be going fucking nuts.

We entered the school district building through a frozen sliding glass door, which had piles of shoveled snow stacked up on either side of it. As we entered, the only temperature difference between inside and outside seemed to be due to the lack of wind.

At the end of the freezing white hallway, two wooden doors slid open, revealing four elderly Japanese men in suits.

Van Guy began chatting and laughing and bowing deeply with the old men, as though having reanimated from his three hours stuck with me. Then, Van Guy turned to me – straight-faced and saying nothing – and ushered me into the room, bowing slightly and gesturing with his cupped hand.

The room flickered and flashed with the flames of an iron stove in the back corner; it was fiery-warm.

The men bowed slightly and repeatedly before sitting me in a small chair at a short table. I felt as though I was sitting at a child's playset.

An elderly woman in a blue and white kimono served tea.

Jude hadn't prepped me for any of this. At least he had told me to wear a suit and tie. It didn't matter. All these guys looked like they had coordinated the same haircut, same shirt, and same suit.

I felt like they were peering at me as though preparing to curiously dissect an alien.

I had no idea the subject when one of them said,
「日本食は好きですか？」

It was translated by another elderly Japanese man: "He say he want to know you like Japanese food."

I crossed my arms in front of my chest and nodded.

"Yes. It's good."

The next question came from another man:

「妻とこどもはニセコに移住しますか?」

It was translated again by the same man: "He say he want to know if wife will move to Niseko."

I looked up at the ceiling and laughed, so that I wouldn't cry. I looked back down at them. They were all staring at me, smiling with anticipation.

What do these people want from me? What is this?

I shook my head.

"I don't know."

"Huuuuuuuuh?"

All four of them had made the noise in unison, raising their voices from a low pitch to a medium-high pitch. The choir-like sound had taken about three seconds to complete. Their group effort would have really creeped me out if I hadn't already been so creeped out.

Next question:

「英語を教えるのは好きですか？」

Translated by the same gray haired, smiling man sitting and sipping tea to my left: "He say he want to know if you like teach English."

I sipped my tea, and it scorched my tongue.

"Yes."

They all stood up, bowed, and left – all except for this man who had translated. He stood right next to me, the top of his head just below my armpit.

"I am the Encho (Principal) Sensai (leader) for the kindergarten. You are – good job. You are now accept. Please buy some jumpsuit. You will not dress like professional now."

It was the first time an adult had looked me in the eye and smiled for nearly a month.

Van Guy took me to my apartment. The moment he opened the door, I thought I would puke.

The place smelled of black toxic mold. I had given numerous seminars on the subject – describing all its dangers, and rights and protections under American law.

I looked at the van driver guy, trying to stifle my gag reflex.

"It smells like mold in here."

He smiled.

"Ah, yes, thank you."

Then he bowed, before backing out of the apartment, bowing again, and shutting the door.

I checked the door to make sure it was unlocked.

I looked around the room.

The 100-square foot rectangle had a wooden planked floor, a tiny kitchenette, and a dirty used mattress in the corner.

They expect me to live in a walk-in closet?

I looked out the tiny window, at that giant Mount Fuji look-a-like in the distance.

I flopped on the dirty mattress in the corner, tears rolling down my face.

I'm a failure in every possible way. I was too weak to stop all this from happening. She talked me into all this, this scam. Now what? Now

what? Now what? She's got us all trapped here...
and it's my fault.

The room slowly faded to black, and time drifted
away –

The Job

15

*T*he next day, Bob and I sat – in the teacher's break room at the school – sipping tea.

Bob

*B*ob, the guy leaving this position, was 26-years-old. He had buzzed orange hair, a jutting underbite, and puffy arms.

He pulled a brochure out of his pocket and slammed it on the table. It looked like it had been in that pocket for way too long.

"Here's a list of all the love hotels on the whole island," he said, smirking.

I scrunched my nose with a crooked smile.

"Aren't you supposed to be teaching me my job right now?"

He furrowed his brow.

"No, you don't really do anything. Just teach English, like, once a week for like 20 minutes."

He stuck his right index finger on the brochure.

"Look, here's a list of all the mixed-gender onsens (hot springs) on the island. You can go there and fuck your wife."

I raised my eyebrows.

"Are you sure you know what it's like to be married?"

He made a happy-looking frown like Robert De Niro.

"Well, I know you've got somebody to fuck whenever you want."

"Really?" I said, "Why don't you teach me how to do my job now?"

He sat back and put his hands behind his head.

"Okay, but nobody really cares about anything here."

I looked down at my new jumpsuit. I looked at *his* jumpsuit; this vomit of blue and black and white Adidas and Nike and Reebok logos.

God, we both look so stupid.

I crossed my arms and nodded.

"That's fine. Still – please show me."

Bob chugged a cup of tea like it was Gatorade, stood up, ran out of the room, and slid on the hardwood floor in the open play area in his socks like Tom Cruise in *Risky Business*, except not at all sexy or cool.

I walked behind him.

Bob threw a toddler on his back and bounced around, then he dropped the child to the floor and dragged him across the wood-planked floor like a mop.

As I followed, Bob stuck his foot out and tripped a toddling child who was running past. The little boy screamed as Bob turned to me and laughed.

I bent over and helped the boy, who must have been four or five, stand up. The boy looked me in the face. He gnashed his teeth, growled, and punched me in the forearm. Then he ran away screaming, his arms flailing over his head.

That was odd. Why did that boy hit me?

Then, Bob went into one of the classrooms and laid on the ground while a swarm of children engulfed him, kicking him in the nuts, trying to jam their fingers in his ass, and punching him in the face.

I just stood there, looking at the chaos with my arms crossed.

What the hell is this?

After a few minutes, he peeled the kids off and ran away, back to the break room.

I followed, feeling like a pet owner trying to keep up with a puppy.

I sat down across from Bob, and said, "Are you telling me that *that* is my job?"

Bob huffed and puffed – his face red and sweaty – looking like he'd just been to the gym.

"What else are you going to do here?" he said, "This place sucks."

"I'm a father," I said, "I would never let my kids behave that way. I'm not going to let little kids kick me in the nuts."

"Well," he said, chugging hot tea, then tossing the empty cup on the table, "basically, your job is to play with them. This is how they play."

"Well," I said, shaking my head defiantly, "I'm not doing that."

He looked at me, snorted, then nodded with a crooked smile.

"Yes you are –"

The next day, a middle-aged woman, who stared ahead stoically, shuffled me into a room where about 30 kids aged three-to-five sat on the floor.

As I turned around, the expressionless woman – in a yellow and white checkered apron – walked out of the room and slid the tan-stained wooden door shut.

I spun back and looked across the room. It was full of tiny faces. They were staring at me in total silence.

Tapping into my "training" I'd received from Jude in Sapporo, I sang *the cow goes moo, and the duck goes quack,* to this room full of Japanese babies. They immediately jumped up, hitting each other, screaming at each other, running in circles, and picking their noses. Within thirty seconds, they were only vaguely aware of the babbling foreigner at the front of the room.

Twenty minutes later, the woman in the apron returned. She slid open the wooden door. When she did, all the children immediately stopped spinning, screaming, running, and hitting. They went to total silence, and ran to their spots on the hardwood floor, sitting seiza (heals to butt).

The woman grimaced.

"Hmph."

Then, she motioned for me to follow her.

She brought me to the cafeteria and showed me how to put lunches on trays, clean up garbage, and close drapes during nap time.

Then I was sat in a baby-sized chair at a baby-sized table, eating lunch with these little kids while they screamed, sneezed, and coughed all over each other, and all over me, and all over my food.

And, that afternoon, they did punch me in the nuts, and they did try to jam their fingers in my ass, and they did slap me in the face.

The kids said that I had no penis; they screamed, with snot dragging from their noses, that I was stupid; one kid told me that I had boobs and then started sexually rubbing my chest; they called me a gaijin; they hit my glasses off my face.

And they did all of this while calling me *Bob*.

So – now I was Bob – just another stupid, white, American dummy to punch.

But I also saw older boys beating the hell out of younger girls; a mentally handicapped girl repeatedly tripped and teased; boys punching each other; teachers grabbing kids by their faces and open-hand slapping them in various parts of their bodies.

The first few times I witnessed these things, I went running to the Encho Sensai, trying to stay calm as I explained to him what I'd seen.

He had responded, with a smile, in slow English.

"What can I do? Thankfully, it is already done."

During nap time that afternoon, a small boy got up and wandered around the hallway. I happened to see him as I left the bathroom. The school janitor went to the small boy, got down on one knee, and rubbed his penis. He asked, repeatedly, if he had to pee. I stopped and stood, dumbfounded, watching this. It continued for at least 30 seconds.

I went to the Encho Sensai. He smiled and said, "Hm. Maybe that boy had to pee. You can just take a break now. It's nap time."

Then, he went into that break room and took a nap himself.

A father came to the classroom that evening to pick up his son. When the boy started flailing and punching, the father grabbed his son by the legs and neck – horizontally – to his waist. Then he dropped the boy to the ground. When the boy got up crying and hitting his father, the man slapped the boy across the top of his head, knocking him back to the floor.

And this happened in front of teachers and students and parents. And everybody seemed to pretend that they couldn't even see it.

Within a few days, it occurred to me that, in an environment where there were no consequences for almost any behavior, there would be no consequences for *my* behavior.

By Wednesday of that first week, I'd decided to learn some Japanese. I started with, *don't touch me*, *don't hit me*, *stop it*, and *no, it's not ok*.

On Friday, a boy poked me in the penis and ran away laughing. I chased him, grabbed him, picked him up, shook him just a bit too hard, and said in Japanese –

"Don't you *ever* touch me again!"

e screamed and ran off –

Niseko Kindergarten January 17th, 2012

Puke

16

*I*began my second week in a battle for my own

mind; a fight to accept the truth… that I couldn't do anything about any of this.

I woke up every night, hacking, worried sick that the black mold I'd found under the sink in the bathroom would kill me, worried sick over my kids down in Misato, and surrounded by townspeople who I had no capacity to even talk to…

And then, on Tuesday – this…

As I sat in a plastic red baby chair, eating noodles out of a plastic white baby bowl at a round baby table, the kid sitting to my left gagged for a few seconds, then puked noodles and broth into his bowl and all over the table.

I was the only one who looked at the mess as the other children surrounding the table continued to eat.

I looked around for something to do about it.

The boy looked up and began to cry.

I looked to my right and made eye contact with his primary teacher. She was chatting with Checkered Apron Woman in the classroom doorway. I gestured with my head to the puke all over the table.

Yuki

由紀

Yuki (You-key) was about my age, in her mid-30's, and had very long bleached orange hair that she had put up in a ponytail.

Yuki – in a blue and white Adidas jumpsuit, fuzzy pink socks, and with a scrunchy on her wrist – entered the room.

I had no idea what she was saying, but she raised her voice and pointed at the mess on the table.

Then, she screamed, pointing that hyperextended index finger at the boy.

"Eat it! 食べるよ!"

The boy froze.

She marched to him, shouting.

"Eat it! 食べるよ!"

The boy shook in his chair, staring at his teacher, his tiny feet dangling.

The other kids ate as fast as they could, their heads down. One-by-one, they dumped their bowls into a black plastic bin, and ran away.

The boy sat, staring at Yuki, his face bright red.

Yuki screamed again, jabbing her index finger into the table with a *thud*.

"Eat it *now!* それを今食べる!"

At this point, I'd completely abandoned any thought of finishing my own food. I was just standing in the corner of the room with my arms crossed over my black and white Reebok jumpsuit.

This kid has hit me. He has grabbed my penis. He has slapped me in the face. As revolting as it is, something inside of me really wants to see this boy eat his puke.

I looked at the mess of goop and slobber and snot sitting on top of his broth and noodles in that bowl. I looked at how the same crap had been projectile-vomited across the table. Now *I* nearly puked.

He began to shovel the mix of noodles, broth, drool, snot, and puke out of the bowl and into his face.

Oh, good lord. Is this real?

Now, *something* else inside of me was revolted. I remembered my daughter.

The boy took another bite, chewing, then swallowing his own spit and snot and puke as he screamed.

He ate another bite.

And another.

And he ate another bite as he screamed.

Oh, God – make it stop.

Yuki now stood behind him with her hands on her hips, lording over the boy.

He gagged twice, then puked into the bowl and the table and all over the place for a second time.

He dropped his chop sticks and his face turned purple as he screamed, teetering in his chair.

Yuki crouched down and screamed at him again, her finger in his face.

His puke, snot, tears, and food now all over his face and clothes and all over the table and floor – Yuki just stared at him.

"It's done おわりますよね," she proclaimed, grabbing the boy by the arm and yanking him from the chair.

She spun him around to face her.

The boy, with his trashed face and hair and red and white t-shirt that said *Oklahoma!* and his tan pants all covered in shit, bowed to Yuki.

He whimpered.

"Gomen nasai ごめんなさい (I'm sorry.)

She grabbed him by the shoulders, shook him, and shouted again.

Now he stood upright – like a soldier or a guard – and shouted.

"Gomen nasai ごめんなさい! (I'm sorry!)

After a group of teachers, followed by the penis-tapping janitor, cleaned the mess, the boy climbed under the table and curled into a ball. There he stayed for the next five hours, until his father came to pick him up.

My sweet little Mae. Oh God help me. If anybody hurts my daughter, I swear I'll kill 'em.

That night, wearing a light-blue mask, I gave up on scrubbing the black mold out from the cabinet under the sink, and did my best to seal it with some insulation tape.

I pulled off that surgical mask I'd picked up at a drug store, coughed my way outside into the snowy rural street, and called Miya.

"This is total *bullshit*. My apartment is full of mold and the teacher made some kid eat his own puke today. What *the fuck* am I doing here?"

She said, "I didn't tell you to go to that place. For Japanese, it's like you're in the North Pole"

I huffed.

"Do you understand what I'm saying? I wake up hacking in the middle of the night! My apartment is toxic! I can't report it because I don't know who to report it to and I don't speak fucking Japanese!"

She shouted.

"That place is so much better than the apartments my dad used to stay at in Tokyo when he was younger! It's much, much better! That's working stuff! You have to sacrifice yourself!"

I paced up and down the snowy road, looking at that volcanic mountain in the distance, the icy snow crunching under my black 1000 yen ($10) boots.

I tried to calm down, and got real quiet.

"The teacher... made... a kid... eat... his... puke... Do you understand me? Do you understand what I'm saying to you right now?"

"I can't do anything," she said, "It's not my fault."

I pulled the phone away from my head, screaming.

"Are Kazuki and Mae getting punched and kicked and molested at school!?? Do their teachers hit them!? *If they do*, that *is* your fucking fault!"

She dropped her voice to a whisper.

"They are doing so good at school. Don't say something like that to them."

I squeezed my temples, trying to smash my brain out of existence, and whimpered.

"Will you *please* bring the kids to see me this weekend? I can't *stand* it. I *can't stand* this anymore."

She scoffed.

"That place sounds awful. We don't need that kind of place."

I closed my eyes and made a fist.

"Miya, what am I doing here? Please, just tell me that the kids are okay..."

She paused for a second.

"You are so weak. This is *your* fault. Nobody told you to go there."

Then she hung up on me –

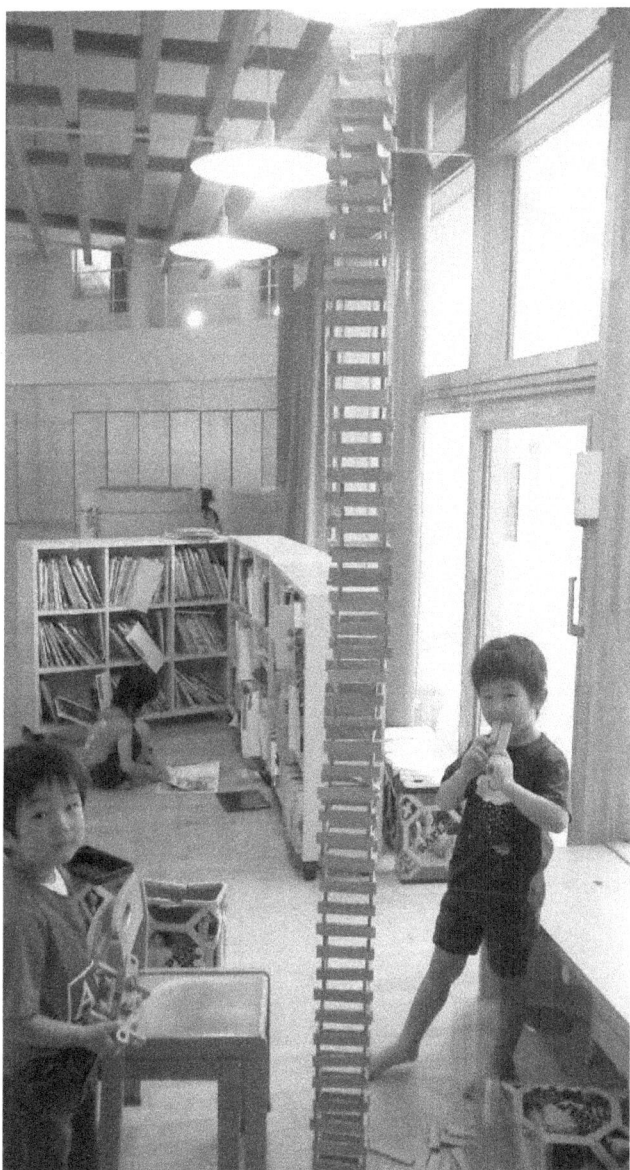

Niseko Kindergarten, February 3rd, 2012

BACK TO MISATO

美郷

Seeking Christmas Salvation

17

*T*he Christmas break started on December

21st.

I took the under-ocean bullet train, arriving in Misato at 8:30 AM on the 22nd. I went up the escalator, turned left, walked through the station – dragging my suitcase to the second-floor elevator – and walked out onto the Misato sidewalk.

I looked up, past the clamoring taxis and buses.

The sky was gray and white, a single cloud from end-to-end. I looked straight ahead (east), and saw a few tiny mountains in the background; they were black, like shadows against the dropping snow. I looked down and gloved my trembling hands, pulling up the fur-rimmed hood of my coat, and grabbing my bag again. Hearing the ice crunch under my cheap black boots, I dragged that bag up the street, into the wind and the freezing rain.

Am I suffocating? Am I exhaling oxygen?

Air was puffing out of me like white smoke; I could see it. My chest felt emptied out, caved in.

Am I caving in? Is my chest collapsing? Am I dying? Am I having a heart attack? I wouldn't even be able to tell anybody.

Black spots filled up my eyes. Waves of electricity shot down my arms. My heart pounded like a trip hammer –

Boom. Boom. Boom. Boom. Boom.

Is this home? Is there gonna be a fight? I just want to see my kids.

Walking down the sidewalk, I tried to pretend the place looked like Minnesota – it didn't.

I opened the front door of the house.

"Tadaima," I said.

Kazuki came running around the corner, plowed into me, and wrapped his arms around me.

He screamed.

"Daddy!"

Miya walked to the entryway and put on her puffy red coat. She glanced at me, as though our arriving in the same place was a coincidence.

"Hi. We're leaving," she said, rushing past me, glancing off the left side of my body.

I kicked off those fake-leather black boots, stepped up onto the raised wooden front entry, and turned back toward Miya.

"Where are you going?"

Miya bundled up Kazuki in a green puffy winter coat.

"We need to get groceries and holidays stuff."

She looked at me for a moment, then zipped up Kazuki.

I just stared into her averting eyes.

Mae came running around the corner. She screamed with a toothless smile.

"Hi Daddy!"

Then, she peeled Disney princess stickers off a sheet, stuck them all over my pants, and ran in circles around me.

Miya corralled Mae and got her all puffed up with winter clothes too.

Mae smiled at me with no front teeth.

Within five minutes, Miya, her mother, and the kids were all gone.

It was 9:00 AM –

The floor creaked as I slinked slowly up the stairs.

"Kentaro?"

I said it, then begged for no response.

I poked my head into the master bedroom. It was empty.

Good – I've gotta find those Passports.

I ran into Miya's bedroom and dug through every drawer. I looked in every bag, every purse, in all our luggage, on the shelf; nothing.

I went back to the master bedroom – to Kentaro and Akiko's closet. I dug through all their clothes, all Akiko's purses, all the drawers; nothing.

I went to the bedroom downstairs and dug through every purse and every bag. I went to the entryway and looked through every shelf. I ran to the kitchen and went through every cabinet, every drawer. I ran to the pantry, the storage room under the stairs, the laundry room, and even the outdoor shed connected to the back of the house; nothing.

I went back to the first-floor bedroom to try again. Then, I caught a glimpse of myself in the mirror propped up against the far wall. I drew my trembling right hand down my face.

My eyes look black; so dilated. My skin is yellow. My hair looks like weeds.

I turned sideways and felt my right arm with my left palm. The arm felt deflated. The hand tingled like it was half asleep.

I noticed my thick black beard and put my hand to it.

No wonder my face itches.

I studied some more, peering into my black eyes, pulling down my yellow cheeks with my fingers and thumb.

Am I dead? Am I a ghost?

I went to the laundry room, found a digital scale, and stepped on it –

53.3 kg. What the hell does that mean?

I took a bath and shaved my beard clean.

I found a kitchen scissors and just started hacking away at my hair in the bathroom.

I went back out to that bedroom mirror and looked at myself again. I didn't look like a ghost anymore. Now I looked like a skeleton.

I dragged myself – utterly exhausted – upstairs, having given up, and laid on my back on one of the futons.

Those passports have got to be somewhere other than this house. Where are they?

I could feel the bottoms of my feet twitch and spasm. I could feel vibrations down the back of my arms.

My stomach turned and turned until I fell asleep.

A few days after Christmas, I sat on that brown couch in the living room, watching *How the Grinch Stole Christmas* with the kids.

I heard feet pounding down the stairs.

Miya came to me.

"You left your computer open. I could see all your emails. I know you have appointment with the U.S. Consulate on February 2st."

On the one hand, we were a family – laughing together, visiting temples, sharing Christmas presents. On the other hand – this.

I had previously conjured a lie for in case I'd needed it. I unleashed it in a knee-jerk reaction.

"I lost my passport and I'm trying to get it replaced."

She crossed her arms and glared at me.

"Hmph, so, where's your visa?"

That was a *really good question*. I couldn't work, or even be in the country without it.

Kazuki started playing with his new Christmas Voltron-looking-thing on the coffee table in front of me. He always dropped his head when we fought.

I exhaled and looked back up at her.

"I lost it. It was in my passport."

Miya, her arms still crossed in front of her, raised her eyebrows.

"If you get kicked out of Japan, I don't support you anything related to kids. You *know* that right?"

That Grinch cartoon, now it looked pretty sinister.

"Yes, I know that," I said, trying to avoid eye contact.

I finally looked up at her.

"You look like you like this. You like this, don't you?"

She smiled.

"I like it. It's much better than in Minnesota. Now I am in charge of everything. I talked to my attorney. That consulate is not going to help you… not at all. Your country cannot help you. They won't help you, at all, from here. I really like it."

She stood over me like a statue, staring at me.

She pointed over at Kazuki and Mae as they watched the Christmas cartoon.

"They don't need you anymore. They are so protected here. When you leave, don't make them cry."

She pointed at Kazuki and Mae.

"If you make them cry, I think you are *really* weak and selfish."

I looked past Miya, to my right, at Akiko dicing food in the kitchen.

I looked back at Miya.

"Yeah, okay."

She dropped her pointed finger and stared at me.

"And I need money before you go. You have lots of money from working."

I turned up my left hand, as if to show her that the amount of money I had in my empty hand was the same amount of money I had in my account.

"I make, like, $2200 a month, and you take most of it."

You're a Mean One... Mr. Grinch, rang out in the background. I looked at the cartoon in front of me, trying to see if I could make sense of the Japanese subtitles.

Miya stared.

"You should get a better job. That kind of job – you could even get vacation, then come here and do nothing for holidays."

I shot my eyes to her as I smacked my right hand down onto the wooden armrest of that couch.

"You know, you should give me back my passbook card... how about that? And the kids' passports, for that matter."

She squinted.

"You should remember it's Christmas time. Now is not the fighting time."

I exhaled.

"Oh, that's good. I didn't know that."

A few nights later, I put the kids to sleep on the futons upstairs.

I read them *Goodnight Moon*, the same book I used to always read them when we were in Minnesota.

Mae patted my face as I lay next to her.

"Daddy?" she said.

"Yes, Peanut?"

"Daddy, why do you look so sad?"

"Daddy has to leave you again tomorrow, Peanut."

"Daddy... don't go. I don't wanna miss you anymore."

Kazuki rolled over, curled up into my armpit, and fell asleep.

I looked up at the ceiling and sobbed in silence.

At 11:00 AM the next day, Miya drove the four of us to the train station.

When I got out of the car, six-year-old Mae came to me crying.

I kneeled down and wrapped my arms around her.

"Bye-bye," she whimpered.

I squeezed as hard as I could.

"Goodbye, Peanut. I love you."

Eight-ear-old Kazuki wrapped his little arms around my neck.

"I don't want to say *good-bye*," he said, frowning.

Miya bent over to little Mae and produced a squeaky baby voice.

"Now is not the crying time. Now is Daddy's working time."

I stood up.

Miya looked at me for the first time I could remember, and spoke in her natural voice.

"Thank you for going away to work. I really appreciate it."

I lowered my eyebrows in confusion.

"You do?"

She leaned over and straightened Mae's dress, zipping up her coat.

"Yeah, I can spend lots of time with the kids like I couldn't do in America. I'm having so much fun."

Ah, great. She's having fun.

Alas, I had to go. There were little kids waiting to kick me in the nuts in Niseko, and my dick wasn't going to kick itself –

BACK TO
HOKKAIDO

北海道

The U.S. Consulate

18

*O*n Wednesday, February 2nd, I took the day off.

I left the apartment in Niseko at 7:00 AM and drove down to Niseko Station, at the base of a mountain. It looked like a white and brown Norwegian gingerbread house.

As I parked in an icy space, Miya called my flip phone.

"The post office keeps asking why I'm withdrawing money from someone else's account whenever I use your passbook card," she said.

I got out of the car, and walked into the station.

"Well," I said, "I guess that's one of the risks you run when you're taking somebody else's money."

She said, "You have to go to the local post office and put my name on your account."

I looked around inside the station for a way to buy tickets, feeling like I was in a vacant theme park.

I said, "I'm not gonna do that. I don't have any money to give you. I'm living off of fucking credit cards. Do you understand that? Why don't you give me back my passbook card?"

She shouted.

"I can say the same thing to you! You make *everything* harder for me!"

I shouted back.

"Alright, great! Thanks!"

I hung up on her by snapping the phone shut, then bought a train ticket from an automated machine.

The commuter train headed north, along the expressway I'd taken into Niseko in that white van back in December. Then it cut sharply to the east, revealing the icy-blue Pacific Ocean on my left, and the rolling landscape of outer Sapporo on my right.

It was surreal. It was dream-like. It was stunningly beautiful. It wasn't fun –

I changed to a local train at Sapporo Station. Exiting that train at Maruyama-Koen Station 円山公園駅, I turned north and headed up the street, my cheap black boots soaking up the snow.

I turned right – peering across the city neighborhood, across Maruyama Park – and spotted an American flag waving a block away.

The consulate was a white compound surrounded by a tall wooden fence. I was surprised at how small it was. It just looked like a flat-roofed church.

I entered the security building, which seemed more like a white manufactured home.

TA single Japanese man represented security.

"What is the purpose of your visit?" he asked in English.

I dropped my bag on the conveyor belt, and sent it through the scanner.

"Passports," I said.

He gestured forward with his white-gloved hand.

"Ah yes. Please, this way."

With a smile, he pointed me to the main building.

American Service Officer Taylor

When I met American Service Officer Taylor, he was standing behind a partition wall and a glass window. He was a handsome man in his early 30's, wearing a gray suit – Italian cut – and a baby blue tie. His neck and back were in perfect posture.

Something about Taylor made me feel like the U.S. federal government was a *good* thing. He looked like an American island sanctuary.

And then he spoke.

"The State Department *cannot* issue passports for a minor without a signature from both parents."

He looked at me, waiting to see if I'd respond. Then, he continued.

"Even if we could, those passports would have no entry stamps. There would be lots of questions about how long your kids have been here and how they even got here. You'd be stopped at the airport."

I said, "Listen, she and I came here to work on this relationship, and we agreed that we'd go back home to Minnesota in April. Without passports, she's got our kids trapped here. She's saying she's going to divorce me and take my kids away...

"Can't you do something?"

He looked down and pretended to shuffle through some papers, an action counter to the integrity I could see inside of him. I saw it in his eyes. I could *feel* it... like my own pulse.

"I'm not sure what we can do about that. It sounds like a private matter," he said.

His eyes still averted down, he slid an English-speaking Japanese attorney's contact information across the counter, through an opening in the glass wall between us.

He looked up at me.

"Maybe this attorney can help."

I stuck my left index finger on the pamphlet and looked him dead in the eye.

"Has this attorney ever successfully shipped foreign children out of Japan?"

He made a modest smile, tucking his upper lip.

"Probably *not*, but he could help you try to get some kind of custody in a divorce."

I inspected his eyes, trying to read them, my eyes darting back-and-forth.

"You mean custody for a foreign man in Japan?"

He nodded.

"Yes. Please keep us informed. I know it sounds trite, but we are very interested in cases like yours."

I gave him back the same modest smile he'd just given me, then slid the pamphlet back under the glass with my index finger.

"I understand your position. I will."

He picked up the pamphlet and looked at me.

I walked outside, and made my way to the gate, scanning my mind for what I would do next.

"Mr. Larson."

I turned around –

It was *Taylor*, standing in his gray suit against the frigid Hokkaido air.

"My boss shouldn't know that we had this conversation," he said.

I crossed my arms in front of my chest.

"Oh yeah? Who's your boss?"

He tilted his chin up slightly, with an inhale, then dropped it again, with an exhale.

"My boss is in Washington –

"There was a case in Fukuoka. The dad had the kids. He got to the front door of the embassy before he was arrested. If you could pull it off where he failed..."

I uncrossed my arms and pointed my gloved left index finger straight west, as though trying to launch myself and my kids back home.

"We were supposed to go back home this spring. Do you know that this country will let any Japanese person take kids from anywhere in the world? Do you know that their government will give them passports? They'll let them come here, and they'll never send them back home! Do you know that?"

His eyes burned through me.

"Mr. Larson, get your kids up here."

I pounded my right fist on my leg.

"That's gonna take too much time! What happens if I get arrested?"

His eyes peered into me, then he looked past me, out past the gate, toward the street. He looked back at me.

"Nothing good. They'll extract a confession from you any way they can."

His eyes turned red and fill up with tears.

I tried to calculate what he was doing, what he was risking. I put my hands on my hips and looked down to the left, as though the answers were on the snowy ground.

"...Taylor... I know it... She's going to take my kids away from me... and she'll never let them leave here."

He pointed at the security building I'd just come through 15 minutes earlier.

"Mr. Larson, that gate right there will be open for you... but you've gotta get past that officer. Then, I'll have to send notice to Washington."

I stood on that frozen walkway, in the gap between two worlds, and pointed at him.

"You're telling me to grab the kids and bring them up here? Wouldn't it be better to just find a way to get me passports?"

"That's not gonna work," he said, "You're not going to get those kids out of this country without an extraction. Bring them here, and refuse to leave until we work out a deal."

He turned to walk away, then looked back at me.

"We'll be here for you."

I shouted.

"Taylor! – Why did you come out here?"

He turned his body around to face me.

"Because I have kids. My wife's Japanese."

I spread my arms wide, as though questioning God.

"And?"

He rubbed his hand over his mouth.

"And this isn't right. *Their* government protects *their* people. I have to try to help you."

He turned and ran through the door, rubbing his arms to warm up.

I left, walking past the officer we'd just discussed as the last obstacle I would encounter after a flight and a bus or an under-ocean train, my wife and the police chasing me.

I walked up the Sapporo, Hokkaido, Japan sidewalk... rubbing the top of my head with my two hands – completely overcome.

I walked back to that little train station, really having no idea where I was. I sat down at a random bench, as random people scurried past, and I held my head in my hands.

My entire body trembled –

Lost in Sapporo

脱出する 19

*H*aving nowhere good to go, I took the train from Maruyama-Koen Station 円山公園駅 back to Sapporo Station 札幌駅.

I took an escalator down, to see what I would find.

Unfolded in front of me was a giant underground city; ticket gates, malls, noodle shops, and bars – I couldn't believe it. It was like Tokyo Station, but new… and very cold.

I must have walked five miles through the white corridor.

I spotted a skinny white guy, surrounded by an ocean of Japanese people, standing in line at a sandwich shop.

I reached up and tapped him on the shoulder.

"You're American, aren't you?"

He said, "Yeah, I'm from Virginia. How'd you know that?"

I said, "I don't know. You just look American. Can we sit at one of these tables and talk?"

He threw his head up and laughed.

"Okay, let's talk."

Ernest

*E*rnest had a drawn face, short brown hair, a goatee, and Clark Kent glasses.

He bit into his sandwich and spoke with his mouth full.

"My wife told me she'd calm down if we moved here. She said she just needed her mom."

After a bite, I opened my sandwich and found shrimp.

"Yeah, mine too," I said.

He shook his head.

"When we got here, she told me she was divorcing me."

I took another bite of this shrimp-ham thing.

"Yup, mine too."

He smiled, glancing across the white underground hallway at the thousands of Sapporo residents rushing past.

"That was four years ago. She still hasn't done it."

I took another bite, still unsure what the hell I was eating.

"How often do you see your kids?"

He put down his sandwich and stared at me. His eyes looking as though they would burst.

"Once or twice a month... for a few hours. They treat me like they're doing me a favor... like I'm being selfish... like I'm bothering my own kids for even wanting to see them..."

His whole face shook and he looked down, rubbing his sleeve across his eyes.

I felt equal parts jealous and determined that I would not end up like him. For a brief moment, looking out across that sea of Japanese people, I remembered that feeling I used to have – that feeling like I could do anything I put my mind to.

"That's more often than I see mine right now," I said.

He leaned back in his chair, and exhaled with a quiver.

"Does yours get violent?"

I put down my sandwich, suddenly disgusted that I was eating a Japanese version of American food.

"Yup."

He looked around, as though checking for spies, then leaned into me.

"I watched her dad chase her down a hill. He hit her across the back of her head, and knocked her to the ground. Everything went flying out of her purse. That's his own daughter."

I looked down at the table.

"Does she break things? Does she ever hit you, or throw things at you?"

He nodded.

"She throws things at me."

I nodded.

"Yeah, mine too."

I leaned it to him and whispered, the hundreds of Japanese rushing through the giant white underground tunnel a few feet from us.

"How many of us do you think there are?"

He furrowed his brow and looked down.

"I don't know. What do you mean?"

I stuck up two fingers as talk and boots and heels and cell phones and laughing clamored beside us.

"I mean, if there are two of us, there could be dozens, or hundreds, or even thousands more of us... people who married into this culture –

having no idea what they were getting into, until it was too late – who've had their lives hijacked."

He looked around as though we were being watched, and sweat beaded up on his forehead.

"Yeah, I don't know. That's too hard."

I leaned back, slapped the small wooden table, and raised my voice.

"Where do people go around here? Is there any place to go out – to meet people?"

He threw back his head and laughed.

"That's easy; Club Booty. There's no cover and there's always cute girls."

I picked up my mystery sandwich and took a big bite.

"Okay, I'll come back here on Saturday. Let's go to Club Booty."

He laughed.

"No. No. I'm still trying to work things out with my wife. That place would make her mad."

I laughed.

"Okay, fine. So, I'll go by myself."

I didn't know if it was true, but I did know that talking to Ernest was the first fun I'd had in months... and, like a starving man getting a small taste of food, I wanted more –

I Wanna Go to America

20

*T*he next Saturday – I did, in fact, show up in

Sapporo. I left the train, took the escalator down to the underground city, and paced.

My brain was buzzing – isolated into insanity – spinning out of control.

Talking to Taylor and Ernest had boosted my spirit, right before having it smashed back down with a building full of screaming babies who hit me and adults who wouldn't even look at me.

Ernest's words had been ringing in my head for a week:

Club Booty

I stood in that underground mall, next to that sandwich shop, and watched the Japanese women scurry past.

High pumps and sparkly things and skirts; I was surrounded.

I wanted to *cheat* –

Damn it! You're so fucking lonely. Go home.

No! I refuse to go back to that apartment to have nightmares about my kids.

I grabbed my hair with two fists and squeezed as hard as I could.

"Grrrrr."

This is gonna be so expensive in so many ways. You cannot do this.

I kneeled on my shins and pounded on my head with the tips of my fingers, then stood up and paced the white hallway of Sapporo Station's underground.

Fuck it. Your life is a nightmare. At least go see if you can meet some people, and talk.

I called Ernest.

"Dude, I'm going to that club. You'd better show up."

He laughed.

"Alright, but I'm not gonna drink or talk to girls."

I bolted toward the staircase.

"Yeah, me neither."

I climbed that stairs, and shot through the bottom floor of a skyscraper. A giant glass door opened with a *blast* of winter air.

I ran up the street, and jumped on a local train.

Susukino, Sapporo, Hokkaido, Japan February 5th, 2012

Off the train and into the flashing ward of
Susukino すすきの – techno music bellowed
through loudspeakers, young people in black
screamed and handed out fliers, girls ran around
in animal costumes, and men in suits stumbled
past.

In the distance, a flashing sign said *Khan's*. It was
a giant building capped with a golden lion head,

like it was on the Las Vegas strip. My directions used that as a marker, so I speed-walked to it.

I turned right and peered into the window of *Rad Bar*. There was a sign out front:

No Cover. Come On In and Get ALL FUCKED UP!

I turned right again and kept walking, pretty sure that Club Booty was close. Two blocks down, I could see a Lawson convenience store, and – across the street from it – a washed out white sign with black letters.

It said:

Booty Bar!

An electric energy burst through me as I pushed open the Lawson convenience store door, and bought three cans of *Super Strong 9%*.

I went outside, snapped them all open, and chugged all of it as fast as I could.

Next thing I knew, Ernest, some Russian dude, and an Aussie were all talking to me –

Ernest put his hand on my shoulder and poked me in the chest.

"Apparently, this guy knows how expensive the drinks are at… THE BOO-TAY BAR!" Ernest proclaimed.

We all laughed wildly.

I said, "Hey! Hey… hey, you guys gotta get somthin' to drink too!"

They all ran into the convenience store and came back out somewhere between thirty seconds and five minutes later.

They all snapped open can-after-can-after-can-after-can of Chuhai Super Strong carbonated vodka.

Ernest piped up.

"Thankfully, drinking outside isn't illegal in Jay-pan."

I flopped my arms around, pointing up the street.

"On the way here… I couldn't find it.. THAT FUCKING lion over there tried to eat my face. That lion's a REAL… FUCK! Fuck that fucking Las Vegas lion! Fuck you lion!"

We all laughed wildly.

"Bwah hahahahahahaha!!"

I pointed again.

"You're not a casino! You're just a Japanese lion!"

I danced on the sidewalk like I was bat shit crazy.

The Russian guy said some Russian stuff.

I pointed, and said to Ernest, "Look, he's a *Ruskie!*"

We all laughed, flapping our arms all over the place on the city sidewalk.

Ernest chugged a can of Super Strong, and slapped me on the shoulder.

"Dat guy teachers En-glish with me."

I squinted in Ernest's face like I was going blind.

"That Ruskie guy? Can Ruskies speak English?"

The Russian guy hit me on the chest with the back of his hand.

"Hey – *American* – some of the girls in there are probably half Russian."

He smiled, really big and crooked.

"Maybe I translate for you... huh?"

The Australian shouted.

"Ay, it's blo-adahy fuckin' cold oud 'ere, idn't it? Let's fuckin'gow."

I slapped all three of them on the back, flapping my finger, pointing across the street.

"L-het's gooo."

The four of us shuffled across the ice-covered street and entered *Club Booty*.

We all shook fresh-fallen snow off our coats, patted our gloves – shooting snow all over – and handed the pile of soaked winter clothes to a heavily-eyelinered woman at the coat check to our right.

There was a smoky dance floor in front of us. Stepping in there for a second, the Japanese techno music thudded through my ears and chest. Ernest pounded me on the back and motioned up the red-carpeted stairs to our right, past the coat check. Up there, the music muffled into background noise. We entered a red room with a bar in the far corner.

Ernest and I sat down in a booth in the middle of the room. Above us, a giant screen flashed videos of people skiing in Niseko. We ordered a pizza and laughed about… something.

I got up to go to the bathroom, and saw two girls sitting a few booths over. They were pointing and looking at me.

I had no idea what they looked like when I put my hand to the back of their booth and leaned in.

"You're prit-ty.." I slurred.

One of them leaned in toward me and put her fist to her chin like the Thinker.

"Hmmm. Are you okay?"

I heard giggling, then went and took a long drunken piss.

As the urinal rocked back-and-forth, I looked at the chipped and cracking red paint on the walls.

I tried to remember what it felt like to be touched by a woman. I couldn't remember. I tried to remember what it felt like to be loved, to be attractive to somebody… to even feel I had any worth of any kind at all to a woman. I couldn't remember. I couldn't think of anything.

Then, as the sink water ran, I looked in the mirror.

You know, you're really not an evil guy. I don't think you are. Maybe you deserve for someone to be nice to you at some point.

I looked into my blue eyes in that beat-up, cracked mirror, and blinked.

Your eyes are not brown. You're American.

Mae's birth flashed into my mind. Miya's whole labor had only lasted about 20 minutes. She was trying to hold in little Mae until we'd made it to the hospital.

The day after they'd come home, I'd made Miya some soba noodles and miso soup. She'd touched my arm, kissed me, and told me it was the kindest thing I'd ever done for her. I couldn't remember her ever touching me again after that. I knew that she had, but I couldn't remember it... nothing.

Smashed glasses, slammed doors, screamed insults, stolen passports, and threats.

I walked out of the bathroom and sat down, across from Ernest, at the table.

The next thing I knew, one of those girls was sitting next to me. She was eating our pizza and drinking our drinks.

I looked over at her. Her black hair must have been three feet long. It was pulled up in a tight ponytail.

Is she old enough to drink that?

She put her face three inches from mine and smiled.

"Hi!"

I looked over at Ernest to see what he thought of all this. He was talking to her friend. He shrugged.

I looked back at this girl.

I slurred.

"Luh-t's go dance!"

She screamed back at me.

"Okay!"

She grabbed me by the hand and dragged me down the stairs and onto that dance floor.

Her hand felt so warm against mine. She spun around to me on the dance floor. She looked into my eyes with a vacant kindness; no past, no hate... just dancing.

So... I danced with her, her long fake finger nails drifting off my palms, Japanese heads bobbing all around us.

Ernest showed up, the house music thumping and the smoke machines spewing.

"Can I dance with you guys?" he drunkenly croaked.

I whacked him on the shoulder with my open hand, and pulled him toward me.

"Dude! I love you man, but you've gotta go fuck off!"

Ernest threw his head back, laughing, and disappeared into the night.

This girl touched my cheek, and turned my head to face her.

"I'm Aoi."

I grabbed her hand and pulled her closer.

"What?"

She screamed over the thumping music.

"My name! I'm Aoi." (Ah-oh-ee)

I shouted back.

"You're *really* short!"

She laughed.

"Yeah, I know!"

I put my face to her ear.

"I'm Dan. What are you doing here?"

She batted her fake eyelashes and pointed at her friend who was now dancing with the Russian.

"My friend told me to come here because she's depressed. She got divorced. I've never met an American before. You're so beautiful."

I looked at the bobbing Japanese heads all around, wondering how they were all so synchronized. Then I looked back at Aoi.

"Your eyes are green. Your skin is so light."

She leaned into my ear.

"These are contacts!"

I leaned into her.

"Huh?"

She shouted.

"My eyes are brown! I'm part Russian!"

I laughed.

"Is that why you speak *English*?"

"No!" she screamed, "I wanna go to America!"

I pointed at the Russian who was dancing with Aoi's friend.

"That dude is Russian! You should go dance with him!"

Aoi shouted over the thumping music.

"No way! I don't like Russians. I like Americans. You're so handsome! Looks like Kevin Costner!"

She ran her fingers across my left forearm.

"Soft."

I leaned into her.

"What?"

She said, "Your arm hair is so soft. It's like a baby."

I shouted.

"I wanna talk to you, but I can't hear you!"

She grabbed my hand.

"Okay, let's go!"

Aoi dragged me out into the Susukino street.

Oh shit... now I'm going to regret doing this if I do, and I'm also going to regret not doing this if I don't.

A cab pulled up and opened its door to offer us a ride. Aoi slammed the door shut and we almost fell over laughing.

She dragged me to a karaoke bar. Inside, I realized that there were two other people with us – Aoi's divorced friend, and some other Japanese dude.

I locked my left hand in Aoi's and pulled her to me.

"I guess your friend didn't like that Russian guy."

The two girls whispered and giggled wildly.

Aoi turned back to me.

"She said that guy stinks."

I looked into her eyes and smiled.

"You know you're beautiful?"

She put her hand on my chest and pulled herself to me, grabbing my arms and wrapping them around her shoulders.

"She said she only wants to talk to Japanese guys now."

She kissed me.

So soft.

I felt her against me, her breasts up against my abdomen. With tunnel vision, I held myself to her, like a teenager trying to make the most of a prom dance.

I felt like my body had floated away.

The Japanese guy tapped me on the shoulder.

"Hey," he said in English, "America, you like Japanese girls?"

I pulled away from Aoi, and the world opened back up.

"What?"

He said, "If you like Japanese girls, you pay."

I laughed.

"What?"

He said, "You and me… we pay for karaoke now. Okay?"

I said, "Okay," and dropped 3000 yen on the counter, immediately wondering how I'd afford food for the next week.

In the closed room, sitting at a booth, bowing service staff brought us round-after-round-after-round of shots and beer and Chuhai.

Aoi she kept touching my leg, and hugging me, and kissing my neck as we screamed Elvis and Rihanna and Eminem.

I upended drinks until the world was spun into a blur.

At some point, we left the flurry of glasses and cans and screams and laugher and flirting – and stumbled out onto the city sidewalk.

The two others suddenly disappeared in some way I cannot recall; drunken magic.

Aoi and I ran around and giggled like school kids on the playground.

Aoi held my hands on the sidewalk and said, "I like you."

I nodded.

"I like you too."

I saw a flash to my right, and the open Pacific Ocean suddenly shined in the distance – the tiny waves flashing brilliantly. The world turned into a deep orange against black shadows, and we walked into a hotel as the rising sun breached the northern horizon.

I shut the hotel room door and looked down at Aoi as she sat on the bed.

I walked past her and looked out the window, down at the day-lit sidewalk.

"Don't you want to go find your friend?"

She grabbed my hand, spinning me to face her, and batted her fake eyelashes.

"What do you want to do?"

I smeared her Egyptian-looking eyeliner across her cheek with my thumb, pulled her mane of black hair out of that ponytail, and took off her shirt.

I love you. I love you. I love you.

I rubbed her forehead against mine, and kissed every part of her face and body. I exhaled with a quiver, as though I'd been holding my breath for years.

Oh God. Oh my God.

...

Oh my God, what have I done?

I woke up four hours later, between white sheets, with an awful headache.

I whispered.

"Hey."

She looked up at me, one of her eyelashes falling off.

She put her hands to my chest and pushed herself up.

"I'll go."

I got up, sat on the corner of the bed, touched her shoulder, and spoke in a raspy voice.

"Yeah, I think you should go. I'm married."

She sprang off the bed, and punched me on the shoulder.

"What? *You* – I really liked you!"

"I have kids," I said, "I have two kids that I love very much. She's divorcing me. She's gonna take my kids from me. She won't let them go back home."

She hit me, and hit me, and hit me.

I put up my hands and blocked her swings.

"Stop – please stop. Just go."

She put her hands on my cheeks, and kissed my lips.

"Soft," she said.

Then, she wrote her phone number on a piece of paper, got up, and left.

I went into the bathroom of that random hotel in Susukino, Hokkaido, Japan and puked in the sink.

I curled up in a ball on the floor until the front desk called and asked me to leave –

Nightmare

21

*W*hen I got to my apartment that February

Sunday afternoon, I found a pink card in the door.

It said:

美哉

(Miya)

The card meant that she had mailed me something, and that it was in the post box downstairs. I set it on top of the cardboard box I'd been using as a table... and just stared at it.

Downstairs is... something... that is going to change my life.

I envisioned page-after-page of divorce documents – all in Japanese – along with notes in English, instructing me where to sign.

I laid on my back on the floor and stared at that card until it was dark outside.

I put on my coat and went into the hallway. I ambled down the echoing staircase, pulled out my post key, inserted it, turned it, and opened the metal door. Inside was a giant cardboard box. I brought it up to my apartment and ripped it open. It was full of vitamins, drink mixes, canned meats, cooking utensils, snacks, and fitness magazines.

I dropped to my knees, crossed my arms over my stomach, and curled up into a ball in the middle of the hardwood floor.

I begged out loud.

"God… please… I can't do this anymore… please either help me or kill me already."

Just then, Miya texted me:

Do you want to Skype with the kids?

I ignored it for a moment, and rolled over on my back, then replied:

Okay.

I crawled to the cardboard box in the corner where my computer sat.

Mae got on Skype and started crying.

"Daddy! Daddy! I miss you! Where are you? Daddy, come see me!"

Akiko came over and scolded her.

"Ganbatte" (gone-bot-teh) 頑張って."

"Fight through the impossible."

I waved my hand like an officer waving through traffic.

"Akiko, please stop. You can go away. It's okay if she cries."

Mae wiped her tears.

"I don't want to cry, Daddy."

Akiko scolded Mae again, and hung up on me.

The screen went black and my daughter was gone.

I got on my knees and pounded my fists into that old mattress. Dust shot up into the air like billowing smoke.

I pounded and pounded and pounded on that bed, then sat down and wrote in my journal as

gray mattress powder rained down all over the
room:

> *If I don't tell Miya I've cheated, I'll be a liar. If I
> do tell her, I'll lose my children forever, even if
> I get them out of here.*

I ran outside, turned right, and looked at the
giant volcanic mountain in the distance.

I texted Miya:

> *I screwed up, Miya, really bad. I'm so sorry.*

She texted back.

> *What did you do?*

I ran to the parking lot across the street, as a
furious wind blasted my face. My car was snowed
in – completely white – and surrounded by ten-
foot drifts. I pounded the frozen door, and pried
it open.

I sat down, slammed the door shut, and stared at
the buried underside of the glass.

I texted Miya:

> *I don't think I can tell you yet, but someday, I
> will need you to forgive me.*

She texted me back:

> *I'll forgive you right now.*

I pounded my forehead into the steering wheel.

I walked back to the apartment and laid on the floor, rolling around, engulfed in flashing visions of death.

And, suddenly, I was on Florida's Gulf Coast. Kazuki and Mae played in the sun next to the ocean.

Little Mae was 20 feet away from me, where the sand met the sea, as I crossed my out-stretched legs. I leaned back and watched her splash around as I felt the sand in my palms and fingers.

I could feel the sun – warm against my face.

Then, out of the right corner of my vision, a dark gray image approached behind her. I sat up as the gray image became a black shadow. It grew quickly in size and speed.

I leaped up and ran as fast as I could, my feet driving through the sand.

"MMaeeee! Nooooooo!"

A great white shark shot up, its open mouth driving toward my little girl.

Mae screamed, running toward me, slogging through the ocean.

"Daddy! Daddy!"

The shark bit down on my little girl.

I screamed as I ran.

"Mae! Mae! Noooo! Mae!"

The shark opened its mouth as it spun to the right. I could see Mae inside, screaming, her little hand reaching toward me.

"Daddy!!"

I ran into the ocean, slogging through the tide, as the shark bit down again, flipping its fins, before swimming off.

I shot up off the mattress as though I'd been electrocuted, and flipped open my phone:

2:32 AM

I rolled around, hallucinating that my daughter was dead.

My brain clanged with noises; that gas heater, the nasty air whipping around the building, the shark, Miya screaming.

I pounded and pounded and pounded on my forehead with my open hands as the sun came up at 4:00 AM, sweat dripping down my shivering back.

I got up and looked out my tiny window.

How can it be snowing again?

I curled up in a ball on the mattress.

Two-and-a-half hours later, I finally pushed myself up, put on a Reebok jumpsuit, and walked to the kindergarten. When I got there, I sat on the floor in one of the classrooms. A little girl came, sat on my lap, and showed me her wooden toy.

An Australian-Japanese boy named Hemi ran up beside me, shoved his entire hand into my mouth, and ran away – his arms squiggling above his head like Grover.

I got up, ran for the bathroom, and washed out my mouth.

Later, Encho Sensai started a game of dodgeball. He didn't try to impose any rules. He decided, instead, to whack some of the wildest kids, looking to me each time with a smile.

So, *I found Hemi*.

I grabbed one of the red balls bouncing around the room.

Hemi came across my vision – from left-to-right – like a slot receiver running a slant route.

I wound up and jacked that kid with that rubber ball right up side his lily-white face as hard as I could.

The ball blasted off his head at a 90-degree angle, and caromed off the wall.

Hemi fell in a heap, his head ricocheting back from the blast.

I walked over to check on him.

After a few seconds, he popped up with a giant red mark across half his face.

When Hemi's father came to pick him up, Hemi ran up to the two of us and screamed.

"Chin chin" (penis).

Hemi's Father

*H*emi's father was a tall, broad Australian man with salt-and-pepper hair. He sold real estate in Hirafu – the Niseko resort area. He reminded me of some of my real estate friends back home.

He sent Hemi away so that he could talk to me, and we walked to the front entrance of the school.

"See?" he said, "Now what the fuck is this penis bullshit?"

I put my hand on my hip, next to the Nike logo.

"These kids talk about penises and boobs all day long."

He scowled.

"I'm bloody fucking sick of it, mate. On Sunday I had a prince in my office – a real fucking bloody prince – from Saudi Arabia. He's got his fucking entourage and the whole thing. I've got Hemi in the office with me. The man asks Hemi how he's doing. Hemi says, *I saw my daddy's penis and I felt my mom's boobs*. He said it in fucking Japanese so nobody knew what the fuck he was talking about, but this is fucking bullshit. This is some bizarre weird backwoods culture, idn't it? Maybe it's time I have a talk with someone here."

I shrugged my shoulders.

"Like who? Self-improvement doesn't seem to be real high up the list of priorities here," I said.

He stuck up his left index finger, his gold wedding band prominent on his fist, and wagged it.

"Well you know what?" It's really fucking simple; there's a difference between *ridiculing* someone and *disciplining* them. There's always plenty of ridicule to go around here, idn't there? But where's the bloody fucking discipline? These motherfuckers, fucking up my kid – maybe it's time I take my kid out of here."

I filled up my lungs as much as I could, then exhaled with a quiver.

"Yeah, I know the feeling –"

AKITA

秋田

Lost in Akita

秋田県 22

*I*n mid-March – resigned that I couldn't get

passports without Miya's signature, and that I had no way to get the kids to the consulate in Sapporo – I requested a transfer to Misato. Instead, my English teacher dispatch company placed me in nearby Akita City 秋田, the capital of Akita Prefecture.

I'd be a 40-mile drive northwest from the kids.

Right after receiving the news, with Niseko socked in by over 50 feet of white walls and drifts, I got the flu.

Hacking and wearing a white surgical mask, I took the underwater train down to Misato.

I spent the two-week spring holiday lying on an upstairs bedroom futon at Akiko's house. My crucial six-month UCCJEA window closed without a word of it spoken between Miya and me. I was too sick; I couldn't fight. I couldn't even move.

I woke up one morning – as the room spun – tried to stand, then laid back down. I flopped my head on the futon, and the world faded to black.

Then, my upper body shot out of bed, drenched in sweat, alarmed that the lights were on. Mae was sitting seiza 正座 (butt to heals) to my left. She was slapping my chest *really* hard.

"Daddy, you have to get up... I wanna play."

Then, she wound up and pounded the middle of my back with her open hand.

Smack!

"Ug," I croaked, exhaling hard.

My eyes filled up with black dots and white stars. My arms and legs tingled. I could feel my heart thumping in my ears and in my arms.

I flopped back down on the futon.

Oh God. Is it a dream? My calves itch so badly. I've gotta dig this crawling stuff out of my skin with my fingernails. My eyes. I'm trapped in this sick body. I've gotta get out of this body.

I turned my head left, against the futon, looking over at Mae.

"Mae, I'm sorry sweetheart, you have to go away from Daddy. I'm gonna get you sick."

My little girl gave me an exaggerated frown and ran away.

I rolled over on my right shoulder, away from where Mae had been sitting next to me, and hacked and hacked.

Miya came pounding her feet up the stairs, and stood in the doorway.

"Get up," she demanded.

I rolled over on my back and looked at her.

"You're too weak to even play with your kids," she said, "so why did you complain about not seeing them in Hokkaido?"

I lifted my head up. She looked like a specter.

She crossed her arms.

"You are just weak. Get up."

Her face looked black and green.

Is she melting?

She stepped one foot into the room and pointed at me.

"You can't even work. You're too weak."

She stepped her other foot into the room.

"I can even divorce you now and take the kids so easy because you are so weak. Maybe next time when you leave here, you will never see them again."

She slammed the door shut as hard as she could, and stomped her feet down the stairs.

Three days later, wearing a surgical mask and still hacking, I picked up my new company-issued car and drove to Akita City, talking to myself out loud.

"Alright, you're here. So far... you've got access to the kids. Think... think... there is a solution. What is it? How can I get them outta here?"

I played an episode of *Seinfeld* on my Mac, and talked to Jerry, Elaine, George, and Kramer as though they were my friends.

An hour later, I saw a blue sign with white letters:

Akita

秋田

I darted west, over rolling green hills drenched with melt water. The road jogged right (north), and the prefectural capital unfolded before me as a collection of homes, rice farms, shopping centers, and a downtown train station. I drove two miles east of that station, and found my apartment, up on the base of a tiny green mountain.

I stepped out of the car, and looked at the forest across the street. Streams of water rushed down toward the city and into the gutters below.

I spun, and looked at my apartment building.

"Looks okay so far," I said out loud, visualizing that I was George... that I was chatting with Jerry at the café.

I hit myself on the forehead with my open palm.

"You're going nuts; stop it," I said.

I opened the door, prepared for the worst. Instead, I found hardwood floors, a kitchen with utensils, a table and chair, and a clean bed. Hell, the place even had a TV and internet.

I couldn't believe it –

I talked to myself some more, wandering in circles inside the apartment.

"Okay, *this* is an advantage. I've got a safe, clean, place – and separate from *Akiko*. This is good. I think this place is good. I think this is good. I'm separate from Akiko. I'm close to the kids. So, this is good. I think this is good. This place is clean. This place is safe. It's clean and I'm safe here. I think I'll be safe here."

Stop it. Dan, this is your mind. You have to stop it. You have to stay sane... for your kids. You have to stay sane. Breathe... you're still alive.

Over the next few weeks, I started working at Akita's five elementary schools. I planned *real* lessons, and *really* taught English, and many of the kids seemed to really like me. They would tell me jokes in English, show me their art work, and ask me to play sports with them.

During recess, a little girl came to me.

"Dan Sensai, asobitai! (I wanna play!)"

"Okay," I said, pushing myself slowly out of the chair.

I followed her to the school's 1970's-looking gymnasium.

One of the kids threw me a basketball. I dribbled for a few seconds, then made a flailing shot that clanged off the backboard.

The kids giggled, slapping my hands, and hugging me.

I was so winded. I put my hands to my knees. I thought I would pass out.

I apologized to the excited kids and went and laid down in the school's second-floor storage closet.

During the next few weeks, I took trips to Misato as often as I could muster the strength to make the drive. Miya had given me access to the kids every time.

On a mid-April Wednesday, though, I felt too dizzy and flustered to drive. I thought that I would, maybe, get lost or get in a car accident. My head felt like it was buzzing – all scrambled. So, instead, I jumped in a hot bath in the tiny plastic tub which overlooked my Akita backyard.

I looked out the bathroom window. There was a stray black cat and a big crow chasing each other in the muddy rice field where green rice was sprouting.

I flipped open my phone and called Miya, steam rising from my red feet, as I hacked up the last of the crud.

"You know, Miya, we were supposed to go back to America a few days ago. You told me we would only be here until spring."

She scoffed.

"The kids don't need America anymore. I'm protecting them."

I watched that cat and crow spinning in circles around each other out my window, then hacked uncontrollably.

"Protecting them from what," I said, "going back to their home country, where they were born and raised?"

Her voice rose up.

"Instead of going back to America, God is going to *get you*."

I heard a click, and she was gone.

I dropped the phone next to the sink, dunked my head in the bath water, got out of the bath, and put on a yukata 浴衣 (Japanese robe).

I walked to the tiny patio off the back of my apartment. White clouds creeped down the valley between the green mountains, as that cat and the crow chased each other. The bird jabbed and snapped its beak and the cat swatted back in the muddy rice field.

I wondered what would happen if they decided they really wanted to kill each other –

Making the Call

*O*n a late April Monday, I got an email from

Taylor, asking me to call him immediately. I wrapped up my English class with some Akita fifth-graders, and texted him:

> *Do you have a way to get the kids up to the consulate?*

He replied immediately:

> *No, but I found something that might work.*

I sped as fast as I could, toward my apartment, as spring melt water rushed down from the green mountains, in the misty rain, all around my tiny car.

When I got to my apartment, I immediately called Taylor.

His tone was measured.

"I found a way to get your kids U.S. passports, but it's not going to be easy."

I made a fist, and shook it.

"Dude! Are you kidding me? That's incredible!"

He sounded like he was talking through his grinding teeth, like Dirty Harry.

"Okay, but – I mean it – it's not going to be easy. You've gotta decide if you want to do this."

I paced the floor, darting back-and-forth.

"Okay, so lay it on me."

"Well," he said, "as it turns out, the State Department can print a minor's passport with only one signature in a particular case; if the passport has been confiscated by a non-American parent in order to strand that U.S. citizen minor in a foreign country."

My mind raced – darting around – and landing on that man in Fukuoka, and on Ernest, and on my question about how many of us there were in this situation.

"Really? Doesn't anybody know about this law?" I said.

"It's unpublished," he said, "I didn't even know about it. But let me finish – someone from the

State Department has to prove that the passports are stolen."

I pointed at... nobody.

"They *are* stolen."

Taylor continued.

"Yes, but it's not that simple. Someone from State has to contact the non-American citizen parent and request the passports be delivered from that parent to the State Department."

I stopped pacing, and closed my eyes.

"Someone from Washington has to call Miya?"

"No, no," he said, "That'd be me. Her refusal to give me the passports will be the evidence that the passports are stolen."

I put my hand to my temples and squeezed, then looked down at the wood-planked floor.

"If she cuts off my contact with the kids, I might never see them again..."

Taylor paused for several seconds.

"...thus, the part where it's not going to be easy. If we don't do this, at some point, you're probably never going to see them again anyway."

Now *I* paused, gathering the strength to say it out loud.

"That's true."

He paused.

He inhaled, then exhaled into the phone speaker.

"So. Do you want me to do it?"

I thought for a moment.

"Yes, I do. *Do it*."

He paused again.

"Do you want to think about it for a day?"

I frowned a big frown and shook my head in defiance.

"No. Do it."

Taylor exhaled loudly.

"Okay. I'll get back to you in a few days."

He called me two days later, on a Wednesday, with that same hesitation in his voice. I ran out into the school yard during the lunch break, and opened my phone.

"– Taylor –"

He said, "Dan... It's done."

I crossed one arm in front of me.

"How did it go?"

He said, "Well – she admitted that she *did* have the passports and that she wasn't, under any circumstances, going to give them to you."

I looked out at the field of sprouting rice across the street, and the smoky green mountains in the distance.

"Do you have any idea where they are?"

He said, "No, I sure don't. She, actually – at one point in the conversation – said that she didn't have them and that they were in a *safe place*. I asked her to mail them to me in Sapporo."

I looked down and kicked a rock on the sidewalk next to the school.

"You know she's not going to do it, right?"

Taylor stammered a bit.

"Sh-she – *well* – she said that she was going to think about it."

I said, "Yeah right."

He said, "Yeah, so I'm confident, at this point, that her goal is to control everything by keeping those passports from you, and to divorce you here in Japan. She told me that she had started a legal action against you that she would not discuss with me."

I looked back, through the big glass doors, at the kids running in the hallways inside the school.

"She's going to get full custody, isn't she?"

"I mean, I think so," he said, 'If we get the final go-ahead, you'll be heading to Tokyo to get the passports. You can ask them about it."

I tried to slow my racing mind.

"So, it's going to be enough to get me passports?"

"Well," he said, "it *should be*. Frankly, I was surprised how straight-forward she was with me. She feels *totally* justified, here, in doing whatever she wants to you."

On Friday, I went to Akiko's house to play with the kids after school – and to test the waters.

When Miya got home, Kazuki and I were kicking a soccer ball in the street. Miya got out of her dad's red Toyota, pointed at me, then pointed at the house.

Not really sure what my other options were, I followed her in. She stomped into the first-floor bedroom, put her fist to her hip, and stared at me. I walked in, and she slid the wooden door shut.

"You know your stupid friend from Sapporo called me, right?" she demanded.

Through the sliding glass door, I saw Akiko go outside, get on her Wicked Witch of the West bike, and ride away. The house was empty.

I crossed my arms and turned back to Miya.

"I told you before, I lost my passport."

She shouted.

"Stop lying! He asked me to give him the kids' passports!

I stepped to her.

"No, you misunderstood it."

She pointed at the floor.

"The kids' passports were sent somewhere!"

I leaned right in her face and *screamed*.

"Where are they!?"

Her right eyebrow twitched.

"I can't tell you. That is American law stuff! I know you're up to something and I know you're lying to me! So many lies! I'm going to protect myself! What are you trying to do to me?"

I pointed at my chest.

"What am *I* trying to do to *you*?"

I slammed the sliding wooden bedroom door open, stomped my feet out to the kitchen, turned around, and jabbed my right index finger at that counter in the kitchen like I was going to put my fist through it.

"When I came here, I dropped Kazuki's passport *right there*!"

She pounded her feet down the hallway, chasing me.

I pounded my feet back down the hallway and met her at the front entry.

"The next day, it was gone!" I hollered.

She leaned into my face and screamed.

"I'm so scared! What are you trying to do to me?"

I stuck my finger in her face.

"Stop asking me what I'm doing! What are *you* doing?"

She said, "I don't show you *my hand*. I already went to the city office and I'm gonna do *something legal* stuff to you so soon!

She crossed her arms and screamed.

"You're *NOT* gonna like it! I even have my lawyer!"

I made a fist with my left hand and shook it in front of my chest.

"I will *never* let you take the kids from me!"

She drove her fists toward the ground and leaned into me.

"Give me *all* your passwords for *all* your Facebook and email and everything, or you will never see your kids again!"

I threw my hands up.

"What the fuck does that even mean?"

She drove her fists toward the floor.

"GIVE ME ALL YOUR PASSWORDS!"

I drove my finger at her face like I was going to punch her.

"Fuck you! FUCK YOU, Miya! You fucking crazy bitch!"

She crossed her arms.

'"God is *punishing* you and He has much more punishment coming to you. What are *you* gonna do *not having your kids*?"

I jabbed my finger at her.

"You brought me here! YOU'RE threatening me! I have NO RIGHTS here! The only question is, *what are YOU gonna do*?"

She dropped her voice.

"Nobody here needs you. You are bothering everybody. You are still young. You should have more kids with somebody else."

The handle on the front door jostled.

Miya and I looked at each other, then looked at the front door.

The door opened, swinging slowly.

Little Kazuki walked in with a soccer ball under his arm. He shut the door, then turned and looked at the two of us.

Miya and I stared at him.

Kazuki smiled a big, toothless smile. He took off his shoes, and walked right up between the two of us.

"Hi Mommy and Daddy."

He wrapped his arms around our legs, and Miya stroked his hair.

Miya and I looked at each other.

I crouched down.

"Hey Kaz. How's it going?"

He scratched my beard with his fingers and thumb, then ran upstairs.

I stood up, and stared right through Miya.

"That was a *horrible* thing for you to say to me."

She crossed her arms.

"Seriously, just go home. You didn't come here to work on it. And don't make the kids cry when you leave – "

Her eyes welled up.

"It's selfish."

She ran upstairs.

A few minutes later, I quietly went upstairs and opened the bedroom door. Miya was laying on the ground in the dark, her arms and legs wrapped around Kazuki. She was whispering in his ear in Japanese.

Taylor emailed me that night:

> *We've got final approval to print passports. You've got to get to Tokyo immediately. We'll only have the State Department's attention for a few days...*

BACK TO TOKYO

東京

The Guards at the Gate

24

*E*xiting the Minato-ku subway station, for a

moment, Tokyo looked like Manhattan. It wasn't new. It wasn't clean. It was nothing like Sapporo. There was litter on the sidewalk. There was rust on the raised train track in the distance.

I felt so... diminished.

It was raining a misty rain. A sea of umbrellas scurried past in every direction. I had no umbrella.

I walked up the street, wiping the water from my face, and found a big brown sign above the sidewalk.

Cars and pedestrians rushed past. Nobody spoke. Nobody honked; not a sound but the rumbling of engines and the rolling of tires against the asphalt.

I tracked the brown sign with my finger.

Holy hell, there must be a hundred embassies…

Canada, Finland, Switzerland, Lebanon, Ethiopia, Zimbabwe, Haiti, Romania, Pakistan, China…

America.

I turned right, feeling like I was going home – like I was going to see Taylor.

I walked up the crumbling Tokyo sidewalk.

After a few blocks – in the distance – I could see a brick and mortar wall, and a big brown sign which read:

The

Embassy of the United States of America

Two blocks away, there was a guard standing before a closed twenty-foot-tall wooden door in a giant, dark-brown wall. He looked like a WWII statue, perched atop a two-foot-square steel crate, and jammed into a white casket-looking thing. The steel crate propped him above the sidewalk traffic while the upright rectangular tent sheltered him from the weather. At this point, he was the size of a G.I. Joe action figure.

I trudged toward him, immediately aware of the passport applications in my backpack.

100 yards away.

I could see the white rifle over his shoulder and the black pistol at his side.

His bouncing image got closer and closer, as I realized that this fight was not all in my head.

80 yards away.

I'm walking toward an armed Japanese soldier.

100 feet away.

Fuck.

Keep going.

80 feet away.

He's not moving. Is he staring at me?

50 feet away.

Is that a real man?

Is that a statue?

Go. Keep going.

30 feet away.

Why doesn't he move? Can he see me? Am I supposed to just walk past him and try to push open the gate myself?

25 feet away.

I can see the whites of his eyes – is he staring at me, or staring past me?

20 feet away.

He's wearing a navy-blue hat and uniform with a white stripe down the leg. I wish he was U.S. Navy.

10 feet away.

 He stepped robotically off his crate and out of his white casket.

I stopped walking and gasped.

He marched to me, as though in a parade, and stepped directly in front of me.

1 foot away.

My head rocked back.

He placed his white-gloved hand in my face, like a traffic cop demanding I stop. His expression was stone-cold.

His white glove still in my face, he spoke English.

"Why are you here?"

I halted.

I inhaled.

I gripped my orange and black backpack with my right hand.

"Passports."

He dropped his hand, pointing me through the gate. His expression was frigid. It sent a chill through my body. I walked to the gate, as he made a call with the black CB box on his shoulder.

The wooden gate opened slowly.

I stepped through, and into the compound.

I turned back to see the man climb back onto the shiny steel box inside of the upright, rectangular tent.

I turned forward and walked up the pavement, wet grass on both sides.

I looked around. 30-foot wall shot up behind me, and on both sides, beyond the wet grass.

To my left, just beyond the gate I'd just walked through, was another guard. He gestured with his white-gloved hand.

"Dozo."

I continued on –

The rain *pinged* off my shoulders.

Fifty feet in front of me, two men stood in the middle of the black-paved walkway, at military attention. The security building was another fifty feet behind them. It was imbedded in another dark brown wall. Then, I could see the embassy, through the mist, in the distance.

I felt like I was ambling into a sniper's crosshairs.

Both men wore blue and white uniforms with white gloves, the same as the guy out front. Both had side arms. One also carried a white rifle. The other had a white stick opposite his pistol.

I approached, smiling with a quiver, like I'd been pulled over.

The guy on the left – the one with the white stick – stomped his right foot, and raised his white-gloved hand to my face.

"Why are you here?"

I exhaled.

"Passports."

They turned to each other at 90 degrees, as though opening a human gate.

The man who had stomped his foot gestured with his left hand and bowed.

「Dozo どうぞ。」

"Please go ahead."

Lightening flashed and the rain started to pound.

I pushed forward again, walking between the two guards, then the fifty feet to the security building. Under the overhang of the rain-drenched building stood four Japanese officers.

One slight man with thick glasses stepped out, placed a white-gloved hand toward my face, and spoke English.

"What is the purpose of your visit?"

I grabbed my backpack as though this man was going to steal it.

"Passports."

He frowned.

"Do you have your passport?"

I nodded.

"Yes, I do."

He winced and switched to Japanese.

「今日はパスポートは作れません。ここにはだれもいません。今日は祝日です。来週また来てください。」

"We are closed for passports today. There's nobody here to help you. Today is a holiday. Come back next week."

I responded in Japanese.

「今日はよーあります。」

"I have an appointment."

He switched back to English.

"May I please see your visa?"

I handed him my passport, which contained my visa. He shuffled through it as though reading my diary with contempt. He turned to one of the other officers and whispered.

He looked back to me.

"Another officer will help you. Please stay outside."

The other three officers disappeared inside the security building. This officer stood with me, holding my passport.

The rain pounded like bullets in my ears. It stopped bouncing off my spring coat, and drenched me, as I stared at this man who stood under the building's overhanging roof.

He stared, blinking.

Rain drops popped off me. I heard them popping – thousands of them.

He stared right into my eyes.

I shivered.

He just stared at me. I wondered if he was trying to look like a shut-down robot.

I stared back at him in defiance, in fear.

Pop, pop, pop, pop, pop, pop, pop of the rain –

Now just glaring at each other –

He slightly looked away as though it was a violation of his duty, but too deep of a human instinct to resist.

The three officers returned, each whispering into this officer's ear – one at a time – each covering their mouth with a white-gloved hand.

The staring officer turned to me.

"Where did you come from?"

America? Minnesota? Misato? Akita?

"Minato Station."

He shouted, for no apparent reason.

"Oh, rain!"

What the hell? Like he just now noticed it was raining?

"Yes, I walked through the rain."

The rain drenched me as I stared at the four officers, three feet away from me, under the overhang, them totally sheltered; completely dry.

Just then, a fifth officer arrived from within the building. He was older, and had a gold badge on his chest that the others did not.

The badged officer took my passport from the other officer.

「あなたはなぜここにいる?」

"What are you doing here?"

I turned up my left hand.

「ぺすぽーと。」

"Passport."

He scoffed.

「パスポートはここにある。」

"You have your passport. It's right here."

I drudged up the best Japanese I could.

「こどーもーのぺーすぽーつもってないです。」

"My children. I lost my children's passports."

He turned up both his hands as though to show me that he was dry under the overhang, while he had me standing three feet in front of him – getting drenched.

「ええ？こどもはどこにいますか?」

"Well, where are they?"

My eyes darted, from left-to-right, across the four others, then I looked back at this man.

「わかーらなーい。」

"I don't know."

Now he switched to English.

"Are your children Japanese or American?"

So – I finally meet them – the people my wife can count on to let her get away with all this shit.

"They're... *American*," I said.

He feigned surprise, jutting his head back, and switched to Japanese.

「今日はビサとパスポートのところにはだれもいません。」

"Today the visa and passport section is closed. There is nobody here."

I planted my feet on the drenched concrete.

「今日はよーあります。」

"I have an appointment," I demanded.

He glared at me with the contempt of a World War.

「誰ですか?」

 "With who?"

I glanced around at the team of officers, all looking as though they were ready to jump me.

I said, 「あーのわかーらない。さっぽーろこんそれーたオフィサーテラーとはなす。だからここいる。」

"I don't know. I spoke with Service Officer Taylor at the Consulate of Sapporo and he said I should come at this time."

The badged officer smiled and switched back to English.

"You spoke with Sapporo? This is Tokyo! Sapporo has nothing to do with Tokyo!"

I stuck my left index finger on the table in front of them.

"Yes, I know. Taylor told me that this *Tokyo Embassy* said I should come here at *this* time."

He turned to the other officers – they all laughed – and looked back to me.

"Okay so give me your appointment letter."

What?

I said, "I don't have one – just a minute."

I stepped back and called Taylor; he didn't pick up –

I snapped my phone shut.

"I don't have a letter. They are expecting me."

He leaned into me with a smug smile.

"Who is expecting you?"

I leaned into him, and put my fists on the table in front of him – out of the rain for a second. I felt I was practically asking him to arrest me.

"I.

"*don't.*

"know."

He switched back to Japanese.

「ちょっと待ってください。」

"Just a moment please."

He stormed back, into the security building, followed by his team of officers.

I stepped away from the table and back into the rain.

The badged officer came back a few minutes later, followed by the other four.

All five presented me with yet *another* officer. This one had stripes across his left shoulder. This man immediately propped open the door to the security building and ordered me in.

On my way in, this new officer took my passport from the other officer, and all seven of us entered the security building.

I went inside that building and immediately realized that I had no idea what these people had in store for me.

I was surrounded –

The building was a fifteen by twenty-five-foot box with windows on every side. There was a big red phone on the wall to my left. And the door I needed to get through was twenty feet in front of me. First, I had to get past a table, a scanner, and six armed men.

Three of them stood and stared at me at attention. The fourth sent my bag through the scanner. The fifth ran a metal detector across my body and patted me down. The sixth – the one with the stripes – stood in front of the door we'd just come through, blocking my exit.

Two of them took an order from Stripe Shoulder Guy. They dumped my bag out all over the table, took apart my cellphone, and dumped out the contents of my wallet.

The two picked up my passport applications and the passport-sized pictures of my kids I'd snapped in the second-floor bedroom in Misato the night before. They held up the tiny pictures, with the unusual-looking cream wallpaper in the background, and stared at me.

The image of those two officers, with their white-gloved hands, holding up those jerry-rigged pictures of my children *seared into my mind* –

Either arrest me or kill me or don't, but get your goddamn hands off my kids.

The light on that red rotary phone on the wall to my left began to blink. Then a hammer clanged a bell inside it. It was high-pitched and loud, like a fire bell.

My breath stopped.

That first officer ran over and picked up.

"Hai. Hai. Hai," he said.

「Hai. Hai. ちょっと待ってください。」

"Just a moment please."

He half-bowed, called me over, and handed me the phone.

Some American woman on the other end said, "Who is this? What the hell's *going on* out there? What are all those officers doing in there?"

I looked to my right. Four of the men were staring at me while the other two collected all my stuff into a white plastic box.

I turned back to the phone receiver.

"I was told to come here right now. These guys won't let me through."

Her voice rose up and pierced through the phone.

"By who? What the fuck is going on out there?"

I raised my left hand and struck a tear from my left eye.

"The Consular Section in Sappor.."

She cut me off.

"What? What consulate? The consulate? Wait. This doesn't make any sense. *Who is this?!*"

The badged officer stepped to me and grabbed my right arm, demanding the phone.

I pulled away.

"It's Dan Larson.*"

She yelled.

"Oh my God! *What!?* Are you out there!? Why aren't you in here?"

I shouted, pulling the phone from the officer, turning away.

"They won't let me in! They've got my kids' passport applications!"

Her voice faded away.

"Go! Go! Go!" she shouted to somebody else.

She came back to the receiver.

"Motherfuckers! They have to let you in! Give that officer the phone *right fucking now!*"

I let go of the receiver as the badged officer grabbed

the phone. I put my hands up as though I'd
dropped a gun –

Officer at Narita Airport October 17th, 2016

The U.S. Marines

*T*he badged Japanese officer put the phone to his ear.

"Hai. Hai," he said.

He hung up, and raised his voice in a shouted one-word command.

「気を付け!」

"Attention!"

The four underlings *snapped* to rigid attention. The Striped Officer crossed his arms, still blocking the door we'd come through.

I saw motion out of the corner of my eye. I looked through the foggy window in the door on the American side of the security building.

A hundred feet away, I saw two African American Marines running in full sprint – *right at me*.

They were a male and a female, both in green-and-gray camouflage fatigues. They both had a sidearm and a rifle, both much bigger than their Japanese counterparts. Both their eyes were covered by pulled-down camouflage hats.

They looked fucking *huge* –

They humped to the door like firefighters diving headlong into a searing blaze.

The Japanese officers were still at stone-wall attention as the man with the striped shoulder peered through me.

The male Marine, with his giant *American Marine arm*, pulled open the door I'd now been trying to enter for nearly an hour.

The two Marines shot through the door, grabbed me – one under each arm – and dragged me through the doorway, dropping me onto the rain-soaked American soil.

The female got right in my ear.

"You okay, Sir?"

"Yes," I said, gasping, "I am now."

On my hands and knees, I blinked in shock.

The young male Marine reached back into the room and clapped his giant hand shut.

"PASSPORT!"

The men stayed at attention – they didn't budge.

The Marine stuck his body through the door, shouting with a flexed rage in his giant right arm.

"GIVE ME THE FUCKING U.S. PASSPORT RIGHT NOW GODDAMN IT!"

That first officer fell out of his pose and began to scramble while the others looked around at each other, trying to ascertain what to do.

That first officer – the one who had stared me down outside in the rain – began to feign reading my passport for the first time.

"Danny-elru Law-som. Hm. Good."

He bowed at a deep 90-degree angle, extending my passport above his bowed head.

Marine Dude snatched it from his hand.

The suddenly short-looking Japanese man looked me in the eye through the doorway separating Japanese and American soil, and bowed again.

"I'm sorry," he said in slow English.

The others collected my things, shoved them into my bag, and handed them all over to the seriously pissed off Marine. He burned his eyes through them all – one-at-a-a-time – then walked away.

The two marines grabbed me under each arm again and pulled me off the grass and to my feet.

The Marine Dude shoved the pieces of my phone into my bag and shoved my bag into my chest.

"Sir, I believe this is yours."

I nodded.

"Yes it is."

We walked up the concrete path through the grass, toward the American Embassy.

I looked at them both, the woman on my right, and the man on my left.

"It's *good to see you guys*," I said.

The Marine Dude whacked my shoulder with his giant right hand.

"It's good to see you too sir."

With a flick of his wrist, he handed me my passport.

We all looked at each other sideways again… and started laughing. The female Marine reached across my back and punched this guy on his giant shoulder, with the glowing smile of American pride.

She looked at me and pointed at him.

"This guy's *pretty good*."

I nodded, never so proud to be an American in all my life.

"Yes he is. You both are," I said.

They escorted me into an expansive American security building, turning right, and marching down the hallway. We walked right through that American security checkpoint, to standing salutes, without even being slowed down.

The female Marine said, "Good luck to you, sir."

I nodded and smiled for the first time in months.

"Thank you, I really appreciate you guys."

The two saluted me, and ran back to their post in a half-sprint.

I walked through the long corridor, and into the Embassy —

The Visa Section

25

*T*he door to the Visa Section was made of

heavy steel, painted brown, making it look more cordial, but – really – it looked as though it was protecting a bank vault.

I pulled open that giant door, walked across the room, and was met with a man. He peered at me from behind a long wall and through a glass divide.

There was a space underneath the glass in front of him, through which he could make exchanges. It looked as though he was selling top secret government movie tickets.

The nametag around his neck read:

> **Principal Officer**
> **Rashida**
> **U.S. Department**
> **of State**

It occurred to me — all-at-once — that, if the kids had been in Tokyo's jurisdiction, I would have never been given this chance. This guy was never coming out from behind that glass.

Rashida

Rashida had a goatee and a bronze pin on his suit lapel where some politicians might have an American flag. His was a United States Shield.

I was a head taller than him. My height over him made me feel awkward.

"Mr. Larson, we've been expecting you," he said, raising his eyebrows.

I threw my black and orange backpack sideways on the counter.

"I was stopped," I said, peering at him.

He said, "Yes, I heard that you had a nice military escort."

I turned to the giant door I'd just come through, then looked back at him.

"I did."

He leaned into the little microphone in front of him, brushing his shiny red tie and his black pinstriped suit on the counter.

"It seems that you are under some extraordinary circumstances, Mr. Larson, and I'm willing to work with you on that."

I took off my drenched black Adidas coat, and tried to unstick the drenched white Nike t-shirt from my body. I looked down at my drenched black Reebok pants as they poured water all over the tiled floor.

"Thank you," I said.

He held up a fistful of documents in a clear laminate folder.

"Now, we do have some paperwork, but Washington has already agreed to provide you with passports for your children, so that's the most important thing."

Rashida slid the clear plastic folder, filled with documents, through the rectangular opening in the glass. I reached into my backpack, pulled out those same documents already filled out, and slid them under the glass.

"Taylor emailed me these yesterday," I said, gesturing to the door to my left with my head,

"Those guys outside – they know I'm here for my kids' passports. They went through my bag."

He looked up from inspecting my documents.

"I want to commend you on your organization."

I stared at him – blank-faced.

He cleared his throat and stood upright.

"You're in here now. For the moment at least, you're in the United States."

I exhaled.

"Okay."

He slid two U.S. passport applications through the space underneath that glass partition. The last time I'd seen this document had been seven months earlier – at home – in Minnesota.

I reached out my trembling right hand to pick up the documents.

I filled out the applications in scribbles, gripping my forearm, trying to stop the vibration.

I raised my hand, and swore it was true –

my spouse is a non-American, she has stolen the passports of American citizen minors, and is using the theft to strand those American citizen minors in a foreign country.

I signed. Rashida raised his hand and signed.

"Now, Mr. Larson. There is a *chance* that you will be stopped at the airport. There could be a few reasons for this…"

He paused for a moment.

"First, the reason could be a call placed to the police notifying them, *this is happening right now.* In that case, you will likely be arrested before you can fly away. Is that clear, Mr. Larson?"

My jaw clenched down.

"Yes."

He looked down, paging through my application documents.

"In that case, the State Department would not be able to help you any further. Is *that* clear?"

"Yes," I said, "I understand."

He went back through the documents, verifying all the required signatures, pointing at each with his index finger.

"The other would be if she notifies – or has already notified – the Immigration Bureau of Japan at the airport that the children are not to leave. In that case, you would swipe these passports, their names would pop up, and you would be stopped."

I said, "I heard they can hold me for ten or twenty days."

He froze and stopped paging through. He closed the application, placed his hand on it, and looked up at me.

"Twenty-three."

I noticed that my stomach hurt so badly that I thought I might vomit.

"Twenty-three?"

He leaned into the microphone.

"Ten, then ten, then three to prepare to charge you with a crime. After that, they usually just release you... Of course, that's not guaranteed."

I looked at the floor.

"Oh God. Okay."

"In that *case*," he said, sliding his hands horizontally, "the State Department would not be able to help you any further."

I nodded.

"Yes, I understand."

He said, "You understand that they can stop you for no reason, then hold you for twenty-three days without ever charging you with a crime? That means no embassy; no Rashida; no Taylor; no consulate; no State Department; no Marines; no attorney. Nothing. Just you and the Japanese police – like those guys you met out there today – in a Japanese prison. You understand that?"

I nodded.

"Yes... I understand."

He took all my documents, stuffed them into a single manila folder, and leaned into me.

"Mr. Larson, Akita would be a very long trip for me to have to come visit you in a detention facility only to be able to do absolutely nothing for you."

I squinted.

"I thought I was in Sapporo's jurisdiction."

He raised his eyebrows and cocked his head slightly like I'd bruised his ego.

"I'm the Chief Officer here at the embassy in Tokyo. Sapporo is a consulate."

I nodded.

"I understand."

He grabbed the little microphone in front of him, and leaned in closer.

"I don't want to go up there."

I put up my hands.

"I got it."

"Now," he said, "if you are handed over for detention, they are supposed to ask you if you want to talk to a consular officer. You are to say *yes*, and nothing further – *nothing*. Mr. Larson, do you understand me?"

I exhaled.

"Yes, I do."

He said, "If they don't ask you, you tell them. They will have to, at some point, call me. You don't say a word in the meantime – *not one word*, no matter what they do or say. Do you understand me, Mr. Larson?"

"Yes," I said, "I understand."

We prepared an envelope to mail the passports to my apartment in Akita.

"Mr. Rashida."

He wrote addresses on the envelope.

"Yes?" he said.

I rubbed my eyes, then looked back at him.

"What if – ?"

He looked up, his brow furrowed.

"*Yes*?" he said.

I crossed my arms over my chest.

"What if – *I don't make it out? What if...*

"What if I can't get them out of here before she does something?"

He dropped the envelope on the counter.

"My understanding is that you have reason to believe that your wife is taking action to sue you for divorce right now. Is that correct?"

I nodded.

"Yes, it is."

"Mr. Larson," he said, "I've been working here in this capacity for many years – many years. *You listen to me*, and you listen to me good."

He put his right forearm on the counter and *leaned* into me as closely as he could, nearly against the glass.

"You *cannot* win here," he said, "You *will not* win here. Eventually, you will lose. And *when* you lose, you will lose *everything*. You will lose all control and all access. You will lose your children. And once you lose, there will be nothing that we can do – that anybody can do.

"You think this was unwelcoming, what they put you through out there today? *Wait until she gets you to court.* They won't… hmph… You have *no* chance. Mr. Larson you have *no chance in court.*"

"I understand," I said.

He put his hand over his mouth, covering his salt and pepper goatee. He looked down and to the right. His eyes welled up red and tears rolled down his face.

"… Sorry," he said, choking it all back, "There've been so many of you guys lately… a lot of you guys… lately… American citizens… who did nothing wrong. Sometimes I can't do anything… Sorry."

I said, "It's okay. I understand."

He pushed his hand further up his face, then brushed it back down, stroking his chin.

"American citizens who *work* on their relationships do better in your situation. We hear a lot about *working on it.* Do you get that?"

I nodded slowly.

"Yes, I've been hearing that I need to *work on it* for a decade."

Rashida dropped his hand from his face and whacked it on the desk with a thud.

"Good. *Do it.* You do it. That guilt stuff... you work on it now. You bow; you praise; you tell her she's a princess; you apologize; you thank her no matter how she behaves. That's your best chance."

I bobbed my head.

"I will try."

He put his fist on the counter and leaned in like a Sergeant knocking a Private into shape.

"You do it."

He inhaled and turned up his nose.

"Do you have any more questions for me?"

I looked at him as steely-eyed as I could muster.

"No."

He turned away before turning back.

"Mr. Larson."

Having stepped away, I stepped back to him.

"Yes?"

He said, "You and Taylor have worked very well together. You keep in contact with him. He can help you."

He smiled through the deep sadness on his face.

"I never want to see you again, okay?"

I nodded.

"You'll know soon enough."

He said, "Have a nice trip back to Akita, Mr. Larson."

He raised his eyebrows and let out a *huff*.

I walked away as he drew a red curtain down over the glass window, ending the day in the Visa section at the American Embassy in Tokyo –

BETWEEN AKITA AND MISATO

秋田と美郷

Fight or Flight

26

*O*n Sunday, May 27th, my plan was to get the

kids out of the house, into a car, 30 kilometers northwest to Akita Airport, through immigration, onto an airplane, *and the hell out of Japan* – at any cost.

The secret flight was at 1:45.

I woke up in Akita and was in Misato by 9:00 AM. As I pulled into the driveway with the tiny black company car, Miya and the kids were about to pull out in the red Toyota four-door.

I waved at Mae as she pounded her little palm against the backseat window.

I looked at Miya. She was wearing a bit of eyeliner with a hint of green eyeshadow. Her black shoulder-length hair was tucked behind her ear.

With ruffled brown mullet surrounding my neck, the vision of her made me feel so ugly. At least I'd found the strength to shave my graying beard that morning.

I tried to blink the floating dots out of my eyes as I looked at my wife.

"What are you guys doing?"

Her voice was low, her face frigid. She peered through me.

"The kids have Track and Field today."

I waved at Mae as she pounded on that window.

"Until when?"

Miya rolled her eyes, looking at the kids in the rearview mirror.

"I don't know."

I put the company car into reverse.

"Okay, I'll come with."

I spun around in the driveway and we both headed to the school.

We were slated to fly to Seoul, Korea, then Minneapolis. And, since it was an international flight, we were supposed to be there two hours early – at 11:45.

Ceremony-after-ceremony at the school – they bowed; they ran; they bowed; they ran; they chanted; they bowed; they chanted; they ran.

I watched the minutes tick off the clock near the roof of the school like my parental rights ticking away.

It was 12:05 when Kazuki ran up to me and shouted.

"Hi Daddy!"

I patted him on the back.

"Hey buddy! Is it done?"

He shouted, jumping all around.

"Yup! I want noodles!"

Back to the house we all went –

12:30.

I went to the kitchen where Kazuki was eating.

"Come on Kaz-man, let's go. Daddy wants to go play."

He looked up at me, noodles falling out of his mouth.

"Are we going bowling?"

I finally got them into the car at 12:45, trembling throughout my body.

With the two kids in the back, I sped up the expressway – through the town, past evergreens, between green mountains – to the airport.

"Hey guys," I said, "we're gonna go to the airport for ice cream."

Sitting in her car seat behind me, Mae raised up her hands and her voice.

"Yay!"

Kazuki looked out the window, frowning.

Taylor had talked me through it:

You are holding passports which say, 'Emergency Replacement of Lost or Stolen Passports.' It's going to look suspicious. Keep the kids calm. Tell them you're getting ice cream. You can explain it once you're on the plane.

I parked and threw the keys under the car.

We went through the automatic doors at the front of the airport, and straight to the ticket gate to our right.

I looked up at the clock on the wall.

1:20 –

*T*here was a young man behind the Korean Air ticketing counter.

He said in English, "Hello sir. What is your final destination?"

I looked up at him with a wild desperation in my eyes.

"Minneapolis."

"May I see your passports?" he said.

I handed over three U.S. passports.

"I see," he said, "and do you have their *Japanese* passports?"

I looked over at his co-worker standing to his right. She was a young woman, with cat eyes and her hair spun up behind her head like it was 1962.

I looked back at him, and heard the *clunk* when I said – "*No.*"

He flinched back slightly. He blinked for just a *split-second* too long, like somebody had flicked him in the back of the head.

He looked at the clock on the wall. He made eye contact with this woman to his right. He showed her the passports. She looked, and tipped her head crooked.

The young Korean man with spiky gelled hair turned back to me.

"Do you have some other kind of ID for the kids, their ko 戸籍?"

Huh? A what? Do I have a what?

His words were squiggles, even though he was speaking English.

I looked down at Kazuki and Mae. Mae looked up at me, smiling.

She screamed.

"Ice cream!"

Kazuki refused to look at me, his eyes welled up with tears.

My guts sank deeper, all of my insides churning.

I looked back up at the young man in the white shirt and red vest.

"A ko... something? No. A *what...?*"

"Ah, *I see*," he said, putting his head down in order to avoid eye contact.

"Mr. Larson, I'm so sorry," he said, looking back up at me uncomfortably, "You have to be here 45 minutes early for an international flight. We cannot let you on this flight."

With a slight tremble in his hand, he put the passports back on the counter.

He and his co-worker bowed.

I huffed in exasperation. I grabbed my chest as my heart pounded and pounded. I looked down at Mae. She was still bouncing.

I looked over at Kazuki and dropped my bag, feeling as though I would collapse and die on the floor.

Kazuki looked up at me, tears streaming down his face.

"Daddy, can we go home now?"

I kneeled down on one knee in front of the Korean Air ticket counter and grabbed him by the shoulders.

"Where's home, Buddy? You mean Minnesota?"

He looked me in the eye.

"I wanna go back to Akiko's house."

I picked up my bag, wiped sweat and tears around my face, and took the kids up to the second floor of that little airport. I found a restaurant that happened to have ice cream.

I opened my laptop, looking for a flight to... anywhere – nothing. We went downstairs to the

ANA service desk, where they told me that no airline would sell same-day flights.

I brought the kids back to the car and kneeled beside them in the parking lot.

"If you guys tell Momma we came here, to the airport, she'll be *really* mad. I don't want Momma to yell at Daddy anymore."

They nodded, blank looks on their faces.

I brought them to the Aeon Mall on the hill to play video games and said, "If anybody asks where we've been, please say that we were at the mall. Okay?"

"Okay Daddy!" they both shouted.

Miya was going to ask, *where were you guys?* Kazuki's seven-year-old reply would be, *we were at the airport!* I couldn't think of any reason he wouldn't say that.

I dropped the kids off at the house in Misato, drove back to Akita, and unpacked – having gone nowhere.

My journal entry said:

> *I didn't make it. I think it's over. I can't fight anymore. I'm never going to see my kids again. I'm ready to die now. I'm ready –*

The Fight

woke Monday morning, May 28th, having slept through the night for the first time since the previous fall.

What happened yesterday? I know I was late, but what was that Korean guy talking about?

It's time to get back up and fight.

I taught two English classes, playing with a sock puppet, and singing the *ABC's.*

I spent the 25-minute recess looking for answers.

Why had we always handed over both U.S. and Japanese passports when we left Japan? Who needed both, and why?

I searched online, digging as quickly as I could. Nothing –

I emailed, asking both my brother Eric – a First Class Petty Officer in the Navy in San Antonio – and American Service Officer Taylor for their opinions. They both emailed roughly the same response:

> *You have passports. You're fine. You're just rattled because you missed the flight.*

No, that wasn't right. I saw it on that Korean guy's face. He had flinched. There was something... something he hadn't told me –

I replied:

Taylor, back in Sapporo, you had told me that I'd be stopped at the airport – why was that again?

Taylor's reply:

No entry information. I'm sorry Dan, this is not my area of expertise.

I wish you and your kids the best of luck.

hat afternoon, I sat in my apartment, the black cat and the crow chasing each other in my back yard, spring meltwater streaming down the tree-covered mountains. Searching the internet, I found case-after-case-after-case of foreigners stopped at the airport with their Australian, British, Canadian, German, Italian, and American kidnapped kids.

They'd been arrested. They'd been held without charge. They'd been beaten up.

What am I dealing with here?

I decided that the Immigration Bureau – *the people who were going to stop me* – knew the answer.

The next day, during recess, I went into the second-floor storage closet. Through the window, I looked down on the kids playing soccer on the wet, black dirt field below.

I closed the door and called the immigration office in Sendai, a distant airport I didn't need.

I got an English speaker, and *lied* –

"My wife accidently went to America with the kids' Japanese passports. We have a flight to meet her there in two days, but I don't know how to get the kids through immigration."

"Ah, yes," she said, "that sounds very difficult. The problem is that they entered Japan on their Japanese passports. Without those, the children will appear to be here illegally. You will be stopped for sure."

I felt my chest heave. I could feel every pulsing vein through my body.

"I *see*. So, how can I solve this?"

She said, "We'll need to get copies of all three of their Japanese passports, take record of their passport numbers, and put a note about this situation into our system. I think you should have your wife call us right away."

I closed my eyes. I held them closed.

"Is there some other way?"

She paused for a moment.

"Ummm... Perhaps you can have her call us as soon as possible."

I could feel my heart pounding, and spread my fingers out across my chest.

"I don't know if she can call."

She said, "So, please give me her phone number."

I said, "I don't know it. Is there anything else we can do?"

She said, "No. If your wife cannot contact us here, and we cannot contact her, I think you will have to cancel your travel."

I turned away from the window and stared at the concrete wall.

"But this travel is very important for us. Is there any other way?"

She said, "Hm. I don't really think this travel is possible until we have their Japanese passport copies and their passport numbers in our system."

I inhaled.

I exhaled.

Okay, Dan, you can do this. You have to do this.

I clenched my jaw.

"But... is there some other way, even if it is very difficult?"

She hesitated.

"Well...

"There is one thing, but, with your wife out of the country, I think that is impossible."

I could feel every inch of my body vibrating, as I stared past the shelf full of school supplies at that concrete wall.

"Ah, so can you please tell me about that?"

She cleared her throat.

"I think it is better if you have your wife call us."

I looked back out the window.

A little girl darted across the black field – from right-to-left – past a group of defenders, and blasted a soccer ball right into the net. Her team jumped and screamed and hugged her.

I made a fist with my right hand, and shook it, trying to force it to stop trembling.

I said, "Because this travel is so soon, I'm very worried. Maybe you can just tell me – in case she cannot contact you – even if it is very difficult."

"Well," she said, "one way to prove that the kids are not in Japan illegally would be to prove that they are Japanese citizens. If they are Japanese citizens, they cannot be here illegally. Does that make sense?"

I shook my head.

"Um. No."

She said, "Our department stops people from leaving if we suspect that they might be here illegally."

I didn't think it was possible, but my head began to hurt even more.

"Seriously?"

"Yes," she said, "If someone is in our country illegally, it must be resolved before they can leave. This way we know, for sure, that they will not have any problems in our country again. Does that make sense?"

No, it sure as hell didn't.

"Uh... yes."

"Okay," she said, "so, what you can do is provide the Immigration Department a koseki tohon 戸籍 ("ko-sek-ee toe-hone") Do you know what this is?"

I said, "Ummm... No."

She said, "Your wife does. I think it is much easier if I speak with her."

I said, "Yes, I will have her contact you...

"...but, just in case, can you please explain this koseki tohon?"

She paused.

"Well, your kids are on your wife's koseki tohon. It is a Japanese family registry document. You are on it too, but this is not yours. So, you cannot get this. It proves your kids are Japanese, but this option seems very difficult, since your wife is already in America."

I looked across the shelves in this storage closet, and found myself fixated on a stack of white printing paper.

"Where did my wife get that document?"

She said, "Japanese have this document registered at our local city office from the time we are born."

I said, "You mean at the prefectural capital city office?"

Her voice turned to a slow kind of hesitant whisper.

"Yes. You would have to get this from your wife. Then you can give it to immigration, and they will *probably* let your children board the plane."

I couldn't stop staring at that stack of blank stack of paper.

"*Probably*?"

"Well," she said, "under our international agreements, our policy is to do that. But, every circumstance is different. We allow our Immigration Officers their own discretion to decide by each case. That is why I want to put notes about your case into our system. I want to make sure you and your kids don't have any problem."

I nodded.

"Okay, thank you so much."

"And what is your name, sir," she said.

I said, "Ah, thank you," and hung up.

_o_I pounded my fist on the shelf in that closet. A plastic bin full of children's scissors jumped, but that heavy stack of papers didn't budge.

I didn't know if I'd been good up to this point or lucky, but I did know this...

1 document down; _1 to go_ –

Akita City Office

28

*T*he morning of Tuesday, May 29th, I booked

tickets from Akita to Minneapolis for that coming Saturday, June 2nd.

That afternoon, I left the school and went straight to the Akita City Office, just west of the train station.

Inside the gray government building, there was a long separating half-wall. Government employees scurried about on the other side.

I went to one of the service desks and asked in Japanese, "May I please have my wife's koseki tohon?"

Akita City Hall, September 6th, 2017

Men and women in white shirts and black slacks scrambled around for 20 minutes. One person asked another, who asked another, who asked another what to do. And each government staff member asked seemed older than the previous.

Finally, a young woman came to me.

"I'm sorry sir, what do you want?"

I said, "I need my wife's koseki tohon."

The woman picked up the plastic white phone on the desk to her right.

"May I please have your wife's phone number?"

I said, "I'm sorry, she is in America."

The young woman went back to an older man and gestured in my direction.

A young man came to me.

"I'm sorry. We cannot give you your wife's koseki tohon. It is a Japanese document."

I said, "My wife is in America and my kids and I need to go meet her. I need it to get through immigration."

For fifteen minutes, they asked each other what to do, gradually building into a cluster of people. It looked a bit like a high-stakes game of telephone.

The young man returned to me, with a slight bow, gesturing down the hallway.

"Please – English speaker."

A woman came down a staircase at the far end of the building.

What am I seeing? Is she American?

City Employee Hafu

*T*his woman wore a pink suit top with her black dress. Her light-brown hair brushed off her shoulders. Her eyes – they were light-brown like Mae's.

She walked to me with a bright smile.

"Your wife has your kids' Japanese passports in America, but you need to travel. Is that right?"

"Yes," I said.

She smiled and nodded.

"I think I can help you."

The woman briskly marched into the office area – behind that separating half-wall – where a cluster of city workers awaited the outcome of our conversation. She went into a tan filing cabinet, ten feet to their right, and came back to me with a single-page document. It looked like a series of rectangles and squiggles.

She handed me the document.

"This is a Koseki Release Form. Please have your wife fill it out, and stamp it with her hanko 判子, then bring it back here."

I squinted.

"Hanko? What's a hanko?"

"Oh," she said, "every Japanese has a hanko. It's her stamp… um… her seal. It's registered here, with this office. It's like a *note-ally*."

I cocked my head sideways and flashed a kind of crooked smiled.

"Note-ally? Oh. A notary! – like a notarized signature?"

"Hai. Um – yes," she said, laughing. "If your wife stamps this, we will give you a copy of her koseki tohon."

I said, "Thank you for helping me so much. You've been very kind to me."

She smiled.

"My father is also American."

I squinted.

"Really?"

"Yes," she said, "He met my mom on Okinawa. Some things like this were… so *difficult.* He is a good man. He had such a hard time sometimes… this kind of stuff. I'm so happy to help you now."

Her face flushed as she cupped her hands over her mouth, then bowed.

I put my trembling left hand to my mouth as tears filled my eyes.

I managed to haltingly say, "Thank you," with a bow.

I ran out of the building, pumping my fist; still alive –

The Stamp

29

On Wednesday, May 30th I shot up out of bed in Akita.

If the Akita City Office knows that my wife is out of the country, but she has to stamp this thing, how would she have stamped it? They know she's not here.

It must be a trap –

Somewhere deep down inside, I knew that my mind wasn't right at all anymore, but I also *knew* that it was a trap.

I left school that day and drove around Akita Station. I remembered having stopped by a 24-hour internet café around there at some point, and that a young woman working there had flirted with me.

I pulled into the lot of that black and orange internet café.

She was there, at the front desk.

I smiled.

"Hi."

She giggled, putting her hands over her mouth.

"Hi!"

I spoke in some combination of English and Japanese.

"Can you please help me fill out this form?"

She gasped, her hands still over her mouth, and spoke in high-pitched English.

"Are you really married?"

"Yes, for now," I said

She put on a pouting frown.

"You looks like Tom Cruise! I *love* Tom Cruise!"

She put her hands over her heart, then filled out the Koseki Release Form while batting her fake, long eyelashes.

I gave her a slight bow.

"Thank you."

She waved and blew me kisses.

"Come back soon Tom Cruise guy!"

I smiled.

"Okay."

I ran to my car, and headed straight to Akiko's house.

I perched myself on that brown couch in the living room, next to the kids, and wrapped my arm around Kazuki.

"Hey buddy, I want to see you on Saturday."

He looked up at me, then back at the cartoon on TV.

"Akiko said *it's no*. I'm gonna go fishing with Gwampa."

I could immediately *feel* Akiko cooking thirty feet to my right. I glanced over my shoulder and watched steam bellow out of the kitchen.

I pulled him tighter to me, and got right in his little ear.

"Well, it's not up to only Akiko. I'm your father, and *I'm* saying we should make a plan to do something together on Saturday."

He looked up at me.

Miya pulled into the driveway, came through the door, marched in front of me, and crossed her arms.

"Mae has dance on Saturday. Can you bring her and drop her off?"

Wow. Okay.

I must have made a pretty weird face, scanning my head for some way to splice what she was threatening to do with what she was actually doing.

I pulled away from Kazuki slightly. He threw his right shoulder up, to push me away, and scooted left. Then he realized he was too close to Mae. So he crawled onto the floor, and into the heated kotatsu futon (blanket-covered table).

I looked back up at Miya. She squinted at Kazuki, trying to figure out his behavior.

I said, "What time is it over?"

"11:30," she said.

Our flight was on Saturday at 1:45 —

"Yes, I can do that," I said.

Okay, I've got Mae.

I leaned forward on the couch, and whacked Kazuki on his little right shoulder.

"Hey Kaz, you still want to go bowling? You want to go on Saturday?"

He spun around on his stomach, under the puffy orange futon blanket.

Miya said, "He's going fishing with my dad."

"Well," I said, "now he's saying he wants to go bowling."

She looked down at him. She looked confused.

I stared at Kaz, trying to *will* him into wanting to go bowling.

The split-second hung in time; I contemplated not being able to get him.

Would I make a run for it with only Mae, as Kazuki fished with his Grandpa?

I thought that I might, but I wasn't sure. The dominos fell in my throbbing head.

Kazuki nodded approval, then spun back around to watch TV.

Miya said, "Well, I guess he's going bowling with you on Saturday. He can go fishing on Sunday."

Miya walked away, and I crawled into kotatu futon with Kazuki.

As dinner was served, I scanned for Miya's hanko stamp in the kitchen which had swallowed up Kazuki's passport back in November.

I decided that I'd better make a backup plan.

I left the house after dinner, and drove up the street. I parked in a random lot, and called Taylor. For a straight-laced D.C. officer, he was pretty pumped.

"I didn't know that you could get out of here with a *family registry document*!" he said, "That's crazy. It's amazing, really. I guess it actually makes sense, in a weird kind of Japanese way."

I said, "So what do I do now?"

He said, "Do you know her maiden name in Kanji?"

I nodded.

"Yup, I sure do."

"Good," he said, "Just go to a stamp store, or even a 100 yen store, buy a stamp with her name on it, and stamp it yourself."

I squinted.

"Yeah, but that stamp won't be registered at the city office, and I'm turning this document into that same city office. If they look it up, I'm screwed."

"If you don't find her stamp," he said, "you're screwed anyway."

So, I went to the 100 yen (dollar) store and bought a stamp with her name on it for a dollar.

I hurried back to the house.

Miya met me at the front door.

"Why don't you go to your apartment? You have work tomorrow," she said.

I said, "I'll get up early and drive to work."

She walked away.

That was odd...

What is she up to?

I waited for everybody to sleep that night, knowing that Kentaro usually woke up at about 3:00 AM.

At 1:00 AM, with my headphones on, the alarm I'd set on my phone went off.

As Kazuki, Mae, and Miya snored next to me on the futons on the floor, I got up and creeped down the creaking stairs in the black of night.

My head and arms and legs tingled all over, like they'd all fallen asleep.

I creeped down the hallway into the kitchen, and shuffled through the kitchen counters and drawers.

I looked over my shoulder repeatedly, slowly opening and closing drawers.

Sure enough, there was the damn thing – in a drawer next to the kitchen table.

Actually, it wasn't Miya's stamp at all. It was *Akiko's* hanko stamp. But, since Miya had never changed her name in Japan, she and her mother still had the same last name.

I went out to my car, which was parked on the concrete driveway and under the steel and plastic car port. As it poured rain, I pulled the Koseki Release Form from its sleeve, made sure the seal wasn't upside down, and I stamped that damned thing.

I went back into the house, placed the seal in its original position in the dining room drawer, ran back out to my car, and drove to my apartment in Akita –

Koseki Tohon

戸籍 30

*O*n Thursday, May 31st, I awoke with a start

and sat up in the western-style single bed in
Akita.

*What if they were just waiting to see if I would
forge this stamp?*

*What if this stamp actually was different from
Miya's?*

*What if I had the right stamp, but it would take
several days to process this?*

*What if, somewhere in the jumbled mess of
Japanese on this document, it said they'd mail it
to me?*

*What if they'd looked up Miya's home phone
number and called her for verification?*

What if Kazuki changed his mind and decided to go fishing on Saturday?

What if I couldn't get Mae out of her dance class early?

Enough noise. Enough fear.

Enough.

I have to push all this shit out of my head and get my kids out of here.

After school, I rushed toward the Akita City Office.

A squad car pulled right up behind me, and I imagined my arrest before he finally turned away.

At the city office, I presented the document to that same young man I'd spoken to before, stamp in place in the lower righthand corner.

"Ah, koseki tohon," he said.

Sitting in a black chair, he glanced at the release form for a split second, before spinning around and stuffing the paper into a filing cabinet. He spun back around with Miya's previously-prepared koseki tohon.

He bowed, while sitting in the chair, and handed it to me.

"Wife's koseki tohon."

"Thank you very much," I said with a bow, and ran away.

I raced back to the 100 yen (dollar) store and bought two dark blue towels, matching the interior of my car, and two big bags I would fill up with clothes.

I'd have to hide the bags, but I wanted to keep my clothes, and I thought I'd look suspicious traveling with no luggage.

Back at my apartment in Akita – once I had the bags in the trunk, I covered them with the blue towels, making things as flush as possible.

I stashed my passport, the kids' passports, the boarding passes, and the koseki tohon under the passenger-side mat.

I went to school the next day, hopefully for the last time, then drove east to Miya's parents' house –

The Flight

31

I awoke in Misato at 6:30 AM on Saturday,
June 2nd.

Kentaro was gone and the kids were sleeping.

Akiko and Miya talked with each other quietly
until I showed up. Then, they looked at each
other and went silent.

So, cold hatred was served alongside hot
breakfast.

I smiled at them both.

"Good morning."

Neither of them looked at me.

After eating, Miya came to me at the kitchen
table.

"You should drive me to the train station."

I searched my mind for any good way to say no.

"Okay."

Going outside, Miya walked toward the back of my car. Seeing that she had three big handbags, I believed that she was going to pop that trunk, where she would have found two bags full of my clothes covered by two car-colored towels.

I had contemplated leaving the luggage in one of the storage lockers at the train station, but timing was going to be my biggest obstacle.

She walked toward the hatch, then – for some reason – she did not pop the trunk. Instead, she sat in the empty back seat.

I got in and looked at her in the rearview mirror. Her head was six inches from my luggage, her feet six inches from the passports, koseki, and tickets.

I put the car in reverse.

"Where are you going?" I said.

"Work," she said.

I pulled out and put the car into drive.

"What are you going to do at work?"

She rolled her eyes.

"Nothing – translating some stuff."

I dropped her off at the train station, and got both kids into the car at 9:30.

Off to dance –

"Mae," I said, "I'll pick you up at 10:45, before your class Is over."

She looked out the window.

"Really? Why, Daddy?"

"We're going to the airport to drop off some luggage and get some ice cream," I said.

She continued to look out the window.

"Okay, Daddy."

I pulled into the dance studio.

Inside, Mae dropped her bag on the dance floor and pulled out her ballet slippers.

When her teacher came by to greet her, Mae said, "I have to leave early! Me and Daddy are going for ice cream!"

The dance teacher's neck recoiled and she made an involuntary noise.

"Heh?"

I'd made a mistake. Taylor had told me to say *airport* after I'd picked her up, not *before*.

This teacher was about to ask where we were going to get ice cream, and Mae was going to say, *the airport!*

I left and took Kazuki to some grocery store to buy snacks for the plane.

As we stood in the grocery store isle, I whacked him on his little shoulder.

"Hey Kaz, did you ever tell Momma that we went to the airport the other day?"

He looked up at me and shook his head.

"Nope."

I squinted at him.

"Why not?" Did anybody ask you where you were?"

He said, "Yup, Akiko did."

I scratched my spiky beard.

"What did you say?"

He reached out his little right arm, squeezed the back of my left arm, and whispered.

"I told her that we were at the mall playing games."

I pulled my head back.

"You did? Why did you do that?"

He stuck out his lower lip.

"I don't know – because you told me to. Let's get candy."

I just shook my head.

On the way back to Mae's dance class, I got lost.

I was trying to keep my heartrate down by pacing my breathing. It was totally not working.

I found Mae's dance class right at 10:45.

As she changed, I asked her if she had told her teacher where we were going.

Mae looked at me with her partially toothless smile.

"Yes!"

I crouched down next to her as she took off her shoes by the dance studio mirror.

"You did? What did you say?"

She glanced at me, then looked down.

"I don't want to say."

We walked out of the studio into the rocky parking lot next to the street.

"Can you please tell me?" I said.

She shouted,

"I said *ice cream*, Daddy!"

So, I had both the kids, and nobody expecting to see us for several hours... and off we went to the airport.

It was 11:30, and Korean Air had said to be there by 11:45 for the 1:45 flight.

Feeling like I was spinning in circles through the green mountains, I suddenly saw a sign for the airport that I could actually read:

Y

I pulled into the airport parking lot at 11:38, and turned back toward the kids.

"What are we here for?"

Mae shouted.

"Ice cream!"

Kazuki looked out the window.

"Is that true, Daddy? I feel sick."

I look at him in the rearview mirror.

"We're doing good, Buddy."

Mae sat up and looked around as I parked.

"Daddy, we're not leaving here are we?"

I went around the car and opened her door.

"No, we're just going to ship some bags and get some ice cream."

At check in, I struggled to write my name on the luggage tags.

They checked my tickets, checked our IDs, and checked my bags before sending us to security.

Kazuki tugged my arm as we went upstairs.

"Daddy, can we go home? I wanna see Momma."

I brought them to the restaurant on the second floor, right in front of security, and got some ice cream.

I called Miya at 12:45.

"I got in a car accident."

She said, "What? What happened?"

"We're safe," I said, "Nobody's hurt. I gotta go."

I hung up.

She called me back several times; I didn't answer.

I took Kazuki and Mae by their hands, and walked – three tickets to Seoul, three U.S. passports, and a koseki tohon under my arm – through security, and to that damned immigration wall.

A man sat in a small glass booth to my left, a closed steel gate in front of me.

I handed him the documents.

"Japanese passports," he said, extending his white-gloved hand, palm up.

I said, 「持ったない。」

"I don't have it."

This man, in black slacks and a white button up shirt with a gold badge sawn into the shoulder, turned up that white-gloved hand like a traffic cop.

「ちょっとまてください,」 he said.

"Just a minute please."

He whispered into the black CB box on his shoulder.

A few minutes later, an unmarked, windowless white door across the hall to my right opened.

A man emerged. He had a gold star badge on his navy-blue shirt.

I checked to see whether he had handcuffs. He did; they were on the back of his belt – no gun.

That first guy stood up and handed this guy the tickets, koseki tohon, and emergency replacement passports.

The guy with the badge sat down behind the desk inside the glass booth and made a call on his walky-talky.

He typed at the computer next to the gate, studying with squinted eyes, then whispered to the guy in the white shirt, who was now standing behind him.

They pointed at the screen, continuing to whisper.

Kazuki tugged on my arm.

"Daddy, what are we doing? We're not leaving here, are we?"

I could see the computer inside that booth, but I couldn't read it.

The guy with the badge typed some more, then he picked up a landline, and made a phone call.

He hung up, then made a call on his cellphone, turning his body away from us.

They're going to arrest me right now.

They're going to hold me until Miya comes to get the kids.

My beautiful babies will come find me when they're adults. I know they'll remember how much I loved them.

I know they'll remember me.

They have to remember me, that I love them.

They have to remember.

Please remember me, my beautiful children.

Remember who I am.

I squeezed their little hands into mine.

he man with the badge stood up, tugging on his badged hat, and walked past me. After glancing at me briefly, he disappeared behind that unmarked, windowless white door across the hallway to my right.

The first guy sat back down in the booth.

A few minutes more —

Japanese and Korean passengers already on the other side of the gate began boarding.

Mae tugged on my arm.

"Daddy, are we gonna get on a plane?"

I looked down into her brown eyes.

"I don't know, Peanut."

My phone rang. I didn't answer. Miya texted me:

> *Send me a picture of where you are. I want to see the car accident.*

The guy at the booth took a phone call from that landline.

"Hai. Hai," he said, then hung up.

The man with the badge re-emerged from the unmarked, windowless white door across the hallway.

He stepped to me.

He presented me with three passports... stamped.

Exit.

He shoved three tickets into three passports, folded up the koseki tohon, and gave it all back to me in a single pile.

"Passports. Tickets. Koseki tohon. Have a good fright."

I exhaled.

"Yeah, *no kidding.*"

 I looked down into Kazuki and Mae's faces.

The man in the white shirt opened the gate.

We boarded that small plane bound for Seoul, Korea, then were told we were delayed for 45 minutes.

I spent every second of that 45 minutes visualizing police storming onboard, on Miya's order.

Finally, we jutted down the runway and took off, leaving Japanese soil, and flying to the safety of South Korea.

Mae bounced around and sang a song she made up about America.

When we landed in Seoul an hour later, I sent Miya an email:

I have taken our kids out of your grip; out of Japan. They are safe and we are going home to America. You can come see them there whenever you want. I win –

BACK TO MINNESOTA

ミネソタ

Flashing Lights

32

I walked up the Tokyo pavement, my heart

racing. I read the brown sign. I turned right, and saw the soldier in the distance. He stepped off the steel crate, out of the white casket, and into the driving rain.

His face flashed with lightening.

In the distance, he threw up his white-gloved hand and shouted.

"Damme gaijinson!"

I charged at him.

"Stop!" He screamed. "STOP! YOU!!"

I ran at him, my raging muscles pumping, charging through the pounding rain, puddles splashing up all around.

Standing in front of the gate, he drew his pistol.

I struck his raised hand away, swiping with my arm, throwing his pistol to the side. It landed, with a splash, on the concrete sidewalk in front of the American Embassy.

I grabbed him around the neck with my left hand, my forearm flexed, squeezing with the rage of a thousand left-behind parents.

I knocked him backward, crashing his head into the wall, and wrapping my raging right hand around his neck.

I dropped him to the right – sliding his body across the wall – to the concrete sidewalk, and climbed on top of him.

My backpack fell off my shoulder, and my pictures of Mae and Kazuki fell out – splashing into a puddle – their images pounded by Japanese rain.

I looked the guard in his eyes, squeezing with both my hands around his neck. Crouching over his chest, I pounded his head into the concrete again and again and again and again and again – pounding his head as hard as I could into that concrete.

He swatted at me with his white-gloved hands, and tried to make a call with the black CB on his shoulder.

I ignored his flailing limbs and squeezed – feeling the power in my shoulders, down into my biceps, and through my pulsing forearms – driving his head into that sidewalk, his hat and his pistol and his nightstick spread out like a yard sale.

Blood poured out of his head and into the water all around, as I looked over at the pictures of my children.

He reached for the pictures with his white-gloved hand.

I squeezed his neck harder – as hard as I could – feeling my heart pumping through my body.

I heard a final gasp.

I tossed aside his lifeless head.

I stood up – over him – frowning, looking into his open eyes.

He's still staring at me.

I picked up my bag, shoving the rain-and-blood-soaked pictures of Kazuki and Mae inside.

I looked back down at the dead guard, the rain pounding on his body.

A tear rolled down my cheek. It blended with the mud and rain on my face.

I threw the bag over my shoulder.

Lightening flashed.

I stepped forward and raised my left hand, looking at the blood.

I turned my hand away, and pushed open the Embassy gate, as the rain stripped away.

I walked into a brilliant light. It flashed white, and consumed me.

I shot up out of bed –

I was in my condo in Plymouth, Minnesota.

My chest was heaving – my stomach and heart thumping and twisted. I was roiling with pain in my arms and legs.

Sweat poured down my back and face.

I looked over at Kazuki and Mae. They were snoring next to me.

I looked at the digital clock on the nightstand:

3:03 AM

I got out of bed, walked to the kitchen, and looked at the calendar on the wall next to the fridge:

June 4th, 2012

I opened the stainless-steel refrigerator door, grabbed a sparkling water, and popped the tab. It sounded like the popping of that Chuhai Super Strong that night in Sapporo.

I heard the Japanese teens shouting and the techno music thumping in the Hokkaido streets. It pounded in my head, more alive than my kitchen in front of me.

I pulled a clean glass from the dishwasher and saw Miya screaming at me that I never did dishes. She took the glass from my hand, smashed it into the floor, and told me it was my fault before running away and slamming the door.

I looked down and saw a fuzzy little figure.

What is that?

I heard – "Daddy?"

I squinted and patted his face.

"Kazuki?"

He looked up at me in red Lightening McQueen pajamas.

I rubbed his back.

"Kazuki – what are you doing up?"

He stuck out his lower lip like he would burst.

"Daddy, can you try to scream a little quieter?"

"Oh son," I said, "was Daddy being loud?"

He nodded with the saddest frown I'd ever seen.

I kneeled down on the kitchen floor and hugged him.

I grabbed him by the shoulders.

"Kaz — I love you sweetheart. I love you so much. I'm so sorry."

He nodded.

"Okay Daddy."

He walked back to the bedroom.

I sat on the tan living room couch, trying to push the flashing images out of my head. The cat; the crow; the bar lights; the woman with the ponytail; that sandwich with Ernest; the mountains; the consulate; those guards...

The images flashed and flashed and flashed in my mind.

I stared through the double-pane sliding glass door, stained with dried rain drops and long-since melted snow.

I stared deep into the darkness —

Passing Judgment

$\mathcal{T}$he next day, I filed for divorce, seeking sole custody.

Miya emailed me:

> *What do you want? I'll do anything to keep my kids in my life.*

I replied:

> *Nothing. I don't want anything to do with you.*

She replied:

> *Can I come there and stay with you and the kids?*

I replied:

> *No. I don't want you anywhere near me.*

Miya stayed in Japan, and – within a few days – counter-sued me for international child abduction.

The guardian ad litem, Angela Manning – for whom this was her last case before retirement – interviewed each of us separately.

As my mind obsessed over Japan, I told Angie that Miya was a good mother, who just had a temper problem. Miya, as it turns out, told Angie that I was psychologically disturbed.

Angie, as it turned out, believed us both –

Over the next year, Miya and I had several court-ordered mediation attempts. They failed. Miya demanded that the kids live with her. I demanded that the kids live with me. Both certain that the other would use any visit to take the kids forever, neither of us would budge.

With all mediations failed, and all hearings failed, it was up to Angie to produce a custody recommendation.

In the summer of 2013, I got the email. I read it while waiting for the kids at a dentist appointment:

> *Given that Mrs. Larson has always been the kids' primary care provider, and given that Mrs. Larson lives with her parents, the*

children will be afforded superior opportunities living in Japan. I recommend that they be relocated there as soon as possible.

I further recommend that Mr. Larson be awarded joint custody in Japan, and that Kazuki and Maya visit him in America each year for approximately eight weeks – subject to the children's school schedule in Japan.

Angela Manning, Guardian Ad Litem

Hennepin County Family Court

I squeezed my cheap little flip phone, scrolled to the bottom of the page, and found her phone number.

After a ring, I heard, "Hello."

"Angie –"

"Mr. Larson?" she said, "I suggest that you get off the phone immediately and have your attorney contact me with any concerns."

"What are you doing?" I demanded, "My kids have spent their whole lives in Minnesota!"

"Oh, you want to have this talk unrepresented? Fine. It doesn't matter where they've lived before," she said, "I have to do what's best for them *now*. They were living in Japan for more than six months. That's their home."

I slammed open the glass door of the dental office, blasted through it, and marched down the Plymouth sidewalk.

"They were in Japan for seven months because Miya stole their passports. And they've been back *here* for 14 months."

She scoffed.

"Yeah, because you kidnapped them."

I clenched my jaw, hard, and pounded the words through my teeth.

"What is wrong with you!? She was going to cut me out of their life! That's what they do over there! Thank God I got them out of there!"

"No," she said, "Miya only threatened to take the kids away from you. You are the only one who actually did it. You have refused any kind of negotiation. We are not going to let you use this court to keep those kids from their mother."

I slapped the window of my blue Prius parked on the curb.

"You have *no idea* what I've been through over there, because you've never asked, and now you're judging me for how I dealt with it?"

She huffed.

"The schools are better there, and Kazuki and Maya deserve access to that culture."

I said, "*Access to that culture?* What, are you kidding me? They won't be *accessing that culture,* they'll be living there... permanently. What about their access to the United States?"

She said, "Mr. Larson... Mr. Larson, this situation is very difficult, and I've checked it all out. This is about the kids. My recommendation is best for Kazuki and Maya."

"Her name is *not* Maya!" I barked.

She said, "Yes, you're right. I apologize."

I said, "Yeah, I know I'm right. I'm her father!"

She went silent.

"Mr. Larson.........

"Please calm down, get off the phone, and have one of your attorneys contact me at another time."

I marched up the street, pointing my index finger in every direction.

"Angie, seriously, you've checked out the schools over there? How? By asking Miya? What about the bullying that that entire culture ignores? Did you ask Miya about the nuclear disaster 100 miles from that place? Did she seem to think that was fine too? And what are you going to do when she never lets me see the kids again, never lets them come here again? You gonna swim over there and save 'em?... Huh? Seriously... Angie... What are you gonna do? Nothing! You can do nothing to protect my kids over there!"

"Mhhm." She said, pausing, "It's like a warning to parents, isn't it? Their sons or daughters marry a foreigner. Then, if they don't want to be here anymore, maybe they want to take the kids and go back home. Then... nobody knows what to do."

I stopped in the middle of the sidewalk.

"Yeah, I think it's a lot more like a representative of an American court recommending American kids get sent to permanently live in a foreign country."

She paused.

"Mr. Larson... why don't you just stop fighting and move back to Japan? Then you can both see your kids, and all of this... is solved."

I pointed my left index finger, driving it forward, at nobody on that vacant suburban sidewalk.

"Solved?" Solved for who? For *you*? So you can make this whole thing go away? So you can retire? Huh? Is that what *solved* means?"

She said, "The fact that neither of you will even consider living in the other's country is not this court's problem.

"I think you moved there, and immediately changed your mind. You sold the cars and everything. Who sells everything, then doesn't move?"

I said, "Somebody under extreme duress."

She said, "Okay, so, you had your moment of truth, and did nothing."

I said, "You know what? I did every single thing I could think of to hold my family together."

She said, "Let me tell you something Mr. Larson. If you take this to trial, all the things you've done – like sending her an email saying, *I win* – are going to come out. Are you really ready for that? Do you really think you can win that?"

I shot back, at her as I paced toward the dentist's office.

"An email!? Are you fucking kidding me right now!?"

I pointed behind myself as though pointing at Japan.

"She stole my kids' passports in a foreign country! That's why they were there for so long! She wouldn't let them leave! She had them trapped there! But I *still* got them out! DO you understand that? Why do you believe everything she says, and nothing I say?"

She said, "Enough of this. Enough. Mr. Larson, get off the phone."

I shook my head, tears flying everywhere.

"I'm giving my kids the first peaceful environment they've ever had in their entire lives. There's no screaming, no threats, there's no broken shit in the kitchen. That's all that should matter."

"Enough, enough. Enough of this," she said, "I have to go."

She hung up.

I smashed my cheap flip phone straight down into the sidewalk with a *pop*. Pieces of plastic shot back up at me, and bounced up the sidewalk.

I stormed into the dentist's office, grabbed the kids – who were now sitting on the couch with bags full of toothpaste and floss – and stormed outside.

On our way to the car, Mae pointed at the sidewalk, pulling at my pants.

"Daddy, you dropped your phone all over the place."

I collected the pieces of phone, got in my blue Prius, and put it back together the best I could. It wasn't helped any, but it turned on.

My attorney, Jolene, called me as I drove the kids back to school.

"Did you see the recommendation that was just filed?"

"Yeah," I said, "I just called her."

"Oh," she said, "and… how did *that* go?"

I looked up at the kids, in their car seats, in the rearview mirror.

"Bad."

She paused, then said, "Um… how bad?"

I slammed my brakes at the stop light at the intersection.

"Really bad."

She said, "What does that mean?

I said, "Really very bad."

She said, "Should I be concerned?"

I nodded.

"Yes, you should."

"Well," she said, "at least Angie's not recommending that you never see them again. She's, basically, just recommending that they go to school in Japan."

I half-smiled.

"Do you think that Angie knows there's no such thing as joint custody in Japan?"

Jolene said immediately, "No I don't."

I hit the gas.

"Does she just hate me, or men, or fathers, or what is this? Why does she just take Miya's word for everything? How can she say that Miya's their primary care provider? Every coach and teacher would say I've been doing everything for these kids since they were babies."

Jolene said, "Dan, I think she's mostly afraid of Miya's attorney. It's like they're all a part of the same club."

I shook my head.

"Pff. Well, that sounds like one hell of a club. Seems like we're not in it."

She said, "Okay, get me a copy of that contract you guys signed back in 2011, immediately – the one that said you guys would return to Minnesota within six months. We're gonna have to fight this thing by proving that you were in a compromised position before you even went to Japan."

I realized, at that moment, that I hadn't seen that document since the night we'd signed it.

"My guess is that Miya has it in Japan, or that it's been destroyed," I said, pulling up to the curb at Kazuki and Mae's school in Plymouth.

"*That is very* unfortunate," she said.

I got out of the car, unbuckled the kids, and walked them up the sidewalk, to their school.

"Yeah, there seems to be a lot of that going around –"

Final Judgment

34

*I*refused to make a deal based upon the

recommendation. So, in mid-August of 2013, Miya flew to Minnesota for a divorce trial.

Judge Clance Berg came to me – in the vacant hallway of the old Minneapolis courthouse building – 60 minutes before the scheduled trial, wearing jeans and a polo shirt.

He walked up, six inches from my face, way too close.

"You *take the deal* where those kids go back to Japan or I'll *make* one for you, and you're *not* gonna like it."

I somehow exhaled and held my breath at the same time.

He pointed his finger at my chest.

"You'll show yourself to be a reckless parent. If I were you, I wouldn't be that reckless with my parental rights."

My head jutted back.

"What?"

He waved that index finger at me, his face still way too close.

"This trial is going to be a big, big, big, big mistake – a huge mistake. If those kids go to Japan tomorrow, I won't lose a minute of sleep."

He turned right and walked into the court chambers.

I went into a side room, and met with my two attorneys. Jolene brushed her platinum blonde hair over her shoulder, then steepled her fingers on the table.

"Dan, he knows that you know sending the kids to Japan with no custody deal will leave you with nothing."

She looked at Matt, my other attorney, then back at me.

"If we start this trial, he could just stand up, claim he has no jurisdiction, and write an order that the kids return to Japan with Miya immediately.

Then, the police – everybody here – will make it happen."

I made two fists and pounded them on the table.

"So, we have to go to trial! At least then I've got a chance."

She grabbed my forearm.

"Dan, he's telling you you're going to lose."

Matt, that other attorney, stood up and adjusted his tie.

"I have never, in my entire career, seen a judge strong-arm somebody like this. I can't believe what he's doing to you. It's just unimaginable."

I said, "We have to go to trial."

I pointed at them.

"I paid you guys tens-of-thousands of dollars to prepare to prove that Angie's recommendation had no legal standing. You guys said it was missing basic information - information it's required to have. You guys said it!"

Matt put his right hand on the table – his fingers spread wide, his multi-colored tie hanging down – and leaned in.

"He thinks he's doing you a favor. You're going to lose."

I put my hands up.

"You guys said this recommendation didn't even meet the basic guidelines. You guys said that we could fight it."

They looked at each other, then back at me.

Jolene touched my hand as it rested on that table.

"I'm sorry Dan. You have no good options."

Just then, through the window of the tiny 7th story meeting room in that Minneapolis family court building, I heard Miya's high heels clomping down the hallway. Then, I saw a flash as she stormed past the window, flanked by two female attorneys.

Miya looked stunning – in a black nightgown, diamond earrings, and a pearl necklace.

I got up, rushed to the door, and threw it open.

"Miya –"

The three of them stopped and turned around, 10 feet beyond me.

"Miya, chotto matte kudasai," I said.

One of her attorneys – a young-looking woman wearing a fuzzy blue sweater – stepped to me, crossed her arms, and turned up her nose.

"Let's try to keep it in English Mr. Larson."

I sidestepped Fuzzy Sweater.

"Miya... I want to talk to you."

Just then, Angie walked past from the other direction. She smiled a big, casual smile – like she'd just served us tea on her back porch.

"Hi, you two. I was just coming by to see how your negotiations were going."

Miya scowled and pointed at me.

"*He* wants to talk to me, but I am not willing to talk to him alone."

I stepped away from the four of them, went back to the room where my two attorneys sat, and gestured with my head for them to leave. They did.

I sat down in the empty room.

In came Miya...

Then, in came Angie.

Angie placed her palms on the table and looked at me.

"Mr. Larson – see? This is what happens when you refuse to negotiate. This is what happens."

I placed my hands broadly on the table, then pointed at Miya.

"She hasn't even spoken to me in more than a year."

Angie took off her librarian glasses, past her pointy nose, placed them on the table, and looked up.

"You won't even consider letting the kids go to Japan to visit their mother."

Miya stood up and pointed.

"I am not willing to talk to him anymore."

Judge Berg came to the small meeting room and opened the door.

"Come on you guys. I've been sitting out here for almost an hour. Are we going to have a trial, or what?"

We all got up and walked out of that tiny meeting room.

I passed my attorneys in the hallway.

Jolene grabbed my left hand.

"Dan, you cannot do this."

I kept walking; she pulled me to her.

"Dan. Dan, you have to listen to me… You cannot win this one."

She looked at me, shaking, tears in her eyes.

"Dan… You're not gonna pull it off this time."

I stopped and just looked at her for a second, her face covered in tears.

I joined a rush of people entering the court room.

Judge Berg, now donning a black robe, sat down next to a wooden gavel, and spun to face us.

"My understanding is that you two have negotiated an agreement based upon the guardian ad litem's recommendations. Is that correct?

He crossed his arms and looked at me with a scowl.

"Yes," I said.

He looked at Miya.

"Yes," she said, smiling.

Judge Berg said, "I hear that little Kazuki likes to golf. Is he going to get a chance to go golfing in Japan with his grandpa?"

Miya smiled.

"Yes… I think so."

Then she stuck out her bottom lip.

"But I'm just *really* worried about Dan's mental stuff. His mental problems make me so worried for him."

I turned to my right and looked at Jolene. She put her fingertips to her forehead and shook her head.

Out of the corner of my eye, I caught my father sitting by himself 50 feet behind me. Looking smart in a suit and tie, tears poured down his face.

Judge Berg said, "Good, so we are in agreement that the kids will move back to Japan. Is that correct?"

I swallowed like I was choking.

Berg looked at me.

I nodded.

"Yes."

Miya nodded.

"Yes."

Berg told our attorneys to work out the details, then got up and left, having never nailed that gavel.

The financials; the travel; the child support – over the next few months, every offer Miya's attorneys made, I refused to sign. Every offer my attorneys made, Miya refused to sign.

So, on a late November Friday, Berg wrote up his own divorce decree and signed it himself. It said that the kids would "move back to Japan" in January of 2014 –

TEXAS

テキサス

Making a Run For it

35

*O*n December 26th of 2013, I packed up our stuff and put the kids in my blue Prius.

I drove straight south, heading to my brother Eric's home in San Antonio.

I was in violation of a court order barring the kids from leaving Minnesota, except for with Miya, in order to move them to Japan the first week of January 2014.

I would ask Texas for emergency jurisdiction, to protect my children.

Miya flew back into Minneapolis, having never notified me when she was coming, and expecting me to hand off the kids. Instead, she was greeted with the news that we were gone.

The evening of December 27th, the Plymouth police kicked in the old wooden front door of my condo and found... nobody.

Driving through Ohio, I received emails from a judge, a guardian, the police, and multiple attorneys – they alternatively threatened me and reasoned with me.

When I arrived in Texas, my brother Eric sat on his staircase.

"Dan, you can't stay here. The Plymouth police called looking for you. They said they've got the Hennepin County Sheriff's department out looking for you too. If you get charged with kidnapping, and I help you, *your* problem is going to become *my* problem. I've got security clearance here."

His two little girls and my two ran around the house like it was a jungle gym.

I looked back at Eric, who still sat atop his staircase.

"Should I take them and go to Mexico?" I said.

He shrugged.

"I mean, you *could*. I think it's gonna suck down there. I think you could just go somewhere up the street and wait for this all to blow over."

I climbed under their dark-stained dining room table as my phone *blinged* with messages from a judge, a guardian, the police, multiple Japanese people living in Minneapolis, and multiple attorneys.

At 2:00 AM, Berg sent me a final warning:

> *I am preparing to notify the authorities that you are desperate and dangerous. If you do not turn yourself in, I will work to issue a nationwide Amber Alert. I do not want your children to see you arrested. I am asking you to do the right thing.*

I laid on my brother's floor in San Antonio, rolling around, my mind spinning with all those flashing lights – the passports; the moldy apartment in Niseko; the cat and the crow in Akita; Ernest.

Then, at 6:30 AM, I got a Facebook message from James Cook. His wife, Hitomi, had proclaimed in my condo back in 2011 that she would take her kids to Japan.

He said:

> *Dan, Hitomi kidnapped our kids. And the whole Japanese community here knows you just took your kids. Don't tell me where you are. Wherever you are, be careful.*

I replied:

> *Do you know where your wife is?*

He said:

She's in Osaka with her mom. Now I'm gonna have to go through Hennepin County to try to get my kids back. Seems like they've got homecourt advantage in both countries, doesn't it?

I sat up, under that wooden table, in San Antonio.

Miya's never going to quit until she gets what she wants...

Something inside me finally overrode my fear of never seeing my kids again; my fear of being charged with a felony in my own country.

At 7:00 AM, with my body convulsing as though I was having a series of seizures, I emailed Judge Berg with Eric's address.

Twenty minutes later, there was a knock on the door.

Eric answered it.

A burly-looking officer poked her head in and found me curled up under the living room table.

"Are you the Dad who took your children?"

I sat up, still under the living room table.

"Yes. The Minnesota court is trying to force me to send my kids to live in Japan."

Eric opened the door further, revealing a young Hispanic man.

He had a gentle, good cop look on his face.

"Are your kids in here?" he said.

I rubbed my eyes.

"Yes."

He shrugged his shoulders and nodded.

"Let's all go downtown and see if we can work this out."

I nodded.

"Okay."

The woman put the kids in the back of her truck, and the man put me in the back of his.

He continued his good cop routine –

"So, what's going on?"

I said, "I've got a guardian ad litem in Minnesota who recommended that my American kids move to northern Japan with their mother."

His eyebrows crunched together, looking at me in the rearview mirror.

His good cop routine melted away.

"Holy shit, dude. Are you serious?"

"Yeah," I said.

He ruffled his little mustache.

"Wow. Dude, that's fucked up."

"Yeah, I noticed," I said.

He frowned.

"Where were they born?"

I looked through the cage between us.

"Minnesota."

He stuck out his lower lip.

"And where do they live now?"

I said, "Minnesota."

He shook his head.

"Dude, what the fuck?"

I said, "They were in Japan for seven-and-a-half months a year-and-a-half ago, but they've been living with me in the condo they grew up in."

He shook his head, like he was looking around San Antonio for an answer.

"Dude... what the fuck? Man, you love your kids, right? Like, you take care of them?"

I nodded.

"Yeah."

We pulled into the underground garage at the downtown San Antonio Police Station.

I was sat in a white room with nothing but a small table and two chairs.

The door I'd entered was closed, and the young Hispanic man opened the door on the other side of the room, revealing a middle-aged white man in a brown suit, a white cowboy hat, and a big gold badge.

The officer gestured.

"This gentleman is the Bexar County Head of Investigations."

I nodded, nearly bowing.

"It's nice to meet you sir."

The two police officers flanked the door as the Head of Investigations and I sat at that little white table.

The investigator patted me down for weapons, then spoke in a long southern drawl.

"You just left Minnesota with your kids?"

I said, "Yes."

He said, "Why?"

I said, "Because I love them and they're being taken away from me."

He leaned back, crossed his arms, looked back at the two officers, then looked back at me.

"You thought you could just come down here in violation of a court order?"

I said, "Well, you guys have a bit of a reputation as the Republic of Texas. I don't want my kids living in Japan."

He grinned and shook his head.

"You seem like a good guy, so I'm gonna shoot with you straight; I'm going to keep your kids here as wards of the state of Texas until your wife comes to pick'em up."

All three of them looked at me – waiting for my response.

I dropped my head and exhaled.

I looked back up at them.

I nodded.

"I understand."

A few minutes later, they told me I was free to go, Kazuki and Mae still with them.

I went outside and sat on the hot white concrete staircase in front of the red brick police station.

Miya and I both got an email from the judge:

> *Miya, Dan has done the right thing and peacefully delivered the kids to the authorities in San Antonio. I want you both to get to Minneapolis by tomorrow morning. Those kids cannot leave this way.*

Attached to the email was a court order requiring that I deliver the kids' U.S. passports to the court the following morning.

As I read the email, the Hispanic police officer showed up from behind me.

"Is the Minnesota court really going to force you to send your kids to live in Japan?"

I stood up, and looked at him.

"Yes."

He said, "To *live* there?'

I nodded.

"Yes."

He draped his thumbs in his pants, around his belt buckle.

"My chief asked me to come find you. Chief wants to know why you told that Minnesota judge where you were."

I furrowed my brow.

"He threatened me with an Amber Alert."

He flashed a crooked smile, showing a dimple.

"They can't issue those unless you're endangering the kids."

I shook my phone, as if to show him.

"He said I was."

He waved his left hand.

"PFFFF! No you're *not*!"

I said, "Yeah, well, that's what I thought."

As the white-hot sun beat down on us, he leaned into me and stuck two fingers toward my nose.

"Chief wants you to know that we didn't care about this Minnesota stuff at all. We all think this whole thing is total bullshit. We would have never come looking for you – never."

I looked away.

"Their mother was never going to quit until she had every single thing exactly her way. I can't win this."

He said, "Do you still have the kids' passports?"

I nodded.

He put his thumb back to his belt.

"Well, my chief asked me to tell you to go get those passports right now, put them in a bucket at your brother's house, and light them on fire."

I heard myself say it.

"If I don't show up with those passports in Minneapolis tomorrow, Minnesota is going to issue a warrant for my arrest. And, she has their Japanese passports. She can just take the kids with those. *It's over.*"

He reached out and grabbed my left shoulder.

"Damn, man, I'm sorry."

He turned, shaking his head, and went back into the police station.

My brother Eric's Mustang came screeching up to the police station curb. He reached across the red and black GT, and popped opened the passenger-side door.

He pounded the steering wheel.

"She's a fucking monster."

I sat down, slammed the door shut, and the car peeled away.

When we got to Eric's house, I went straight to my Prius. I reached inside and grabbed Mae's giant stuffed bear we'd named "Barely." I laid down on the Texas-crabgrass-lawn, and squeezed Barely, staring at the high blue sky.

My brother's Filipino wife, Abigail, showed up.

"Dan, are you okay?"

I said, "No."

She leaned over, with this soft look on her face.

"Okay, well you lay there and roll around in the grass or whatever for a while, then you come in and be Uncle Dan for my kids."

She patted the front of my shoulder as I laid on my back in her crabgrass.

"We'll get some food in you and get you to the airport. We found a flight to Minneapolis. It's in three hours," she said.

20 minutes later, I finally did drop that bear.

At the airport gate, waiting to fly back to Minnesota – probably to be arrested – I thought I heard Mae.

"Hi Daddy."

I turned around. It *was* Mae. She and Kazuki were being physically blocked from me and shuffled away, around the corner, by Miya.

Kazuki looked at me, laughing.

"Hey Daddy, we're all on the same plane!"

Throughout the flight, I heard Mae shout to me from six rows back.

"Daddy, are you still up there?" "Daddy, can we color?" "Daddy, come sit with me."

Miya was trying to keep Mae quiet, and it was totally not working.

The following morning, Miya and I sat in front of Judge Berg.

He darted his head back-and-forth at both of us.

"Well, it was a long night for all of us, but we have *got* to get some success here. Mr. Larson should spend some court-supervised time with his kids at the Mall of America so that you can all say goodbye."

A few hours later, at the Mall of America, I hugged Kazuki and Mae for one last time, and the guardian ad litem shuffled me off in the opposite direction.

Their laughs, their smiles, their dancing, their little faces...

They were gone...

I went back to my silent condo in Plymouth, where the door was kicked in, and curled into a ball on the tan leather couch –

BACK TO

JAPAN

日本

They Can't

36

*I*t was August of 2016, and the agent at the

Minneapolis International Airport printed out two plane tickets and a gate pass.

She looked down at Kazuki and Mae with big eyes.

"Wow, what a big trip. You guys get to go to Japan! You're so lucky. How long will you be there?"

I said, "They were just here with me for a few weeks… so."

Now Kazuki's eyes bugged out.

"We live there."

Mae hit him on the arm *really* hard.

He yelled, turning to look at me.

"Ouch!"

Mae wrinkled her nose.

"No, we don't!"

Then she put her little right hand on her little right hip.

"We live there *and* here!"

The ticket agent squinted, and cocked her head sideways.

I tapped my left hand on the counter.

"They live there… with their mother."

Mae slapped my right arm repeatedly.

"Daddy, you have lots of meat on your arms. You are stronger than Kazuki. He is so weak."

The woman squinted.

"Sorry, it's none of my business, but – if you don't mind my asking – what *is* this?"

I shook my head and said, "I'll be heading back to Japan to see them in four months."

The woman shook her head.

"Wow. This is crazy. But they both speak English. Where were they born?"

I said, "Right here."

She shook her head even more vigorously.

"Did you, like, agree to this?"

I shook my head.

"No, I sure didn't. Hennepin County forced me into this."

Her eyebrows pressed together and down in disgust.

"Well... they can't do that."

I said, "Oh yes they can."

She crossed her arms and leaned back.

"How? How did this happen?"

I nodded.

"Exactly. It's a long story."

She placed the two one-way tickets to Japan and the gate pass on the counter, continuing to look at me and shake her head.

"When you're there... like, how does that work? Do you... see them?"

I said, "You know, their mother never did do one single thing to stop me from seeing them."

She crossed her arms and looked me in the eyes as though scanning for answers inside my soul.

"Well, still, that is a *really* long time without your kids... and they're little! I need to see my kids every day. How do you deal with *that*?"

I couldn't help it, knowing my kids were about to get on that giant plane all by themselves and just fly away, my eyes finally did well up with tears.

I said, "I don't know."

I reached to pick up the tickets.

The woman placed her left hand on top of mine, and smiled a trembling smile.

"I've never heard of anything like this before in my life. This is awful. This is insane."

I looked down, into Kazuki and Mae's little faces, then turned back to this woman.

"Well," I said, "we still have our kids. They're alive. They have dance, and karate, and piano, and band. It's just that it's all in Japan.

"That's really all I have left that I can say about it —"

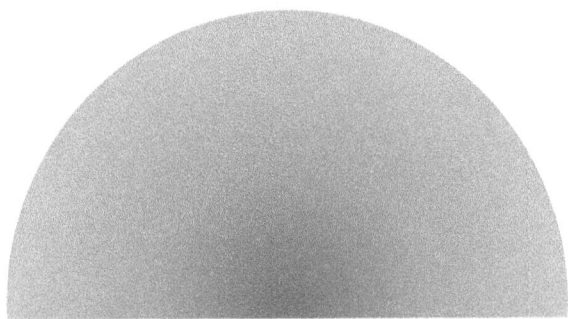

終わり

In April of 2014, Japan joined the Hague Convention on the Civil Aspects of International Child Abduction. Hundreds of parents are still missing their children inside of Japan.

I see my children about seven weeks per year.

In a way, I'm one of the lucky ones...

To my beautiful children – I am so sorry that I could not have done all this better. Daddy did the best that he could. It wasn't good enough.

Daddy loves you –

*Dedicated to those loving parents who have lost
years with their children, including Miya.*

www.ingramcontent.com/pod-product-compliance
Lightning Source LLC
LaVergne TN
LVHW091212080426
835509LV00009B/955